VARIATIONS
COOKBOOK
VEGETABLES

Abbreviations and Quantities

1 oz	= 1 ounce = 28 grams
1 lb	= 1 pound = 16 ounces
1 cup	= approx. 5-8 ounces * (depending on density)
1 cup	= 8 fluid ounces = 250 milliliters (liquids)
2 cups	= 1 pint (liquids)
8 pints	= 4 quarts = 1 gallon (liquids)
1 g	= 1 gram = $\frac{1}{1000}$ kilogram
1 kg	= 1 kilogram = 1000 grams = $2\frac{1}{4}$ lb
1 l	= 1 liter = 1000 milliliters (ml) = approx. 34 fluid ounces
125 milliliters (ml)	= approx. 8 tablespoons = $\frac{1}{2}$ cup
1 tbsp	= 1 level tablespoon = 15-20 g * (depending on density); = 15 milliliters (liquids)
1 tsp	= 1 level teaspoon = 3-5 g * (depending on density) = 5 ml (liquids)

*The weight of dry ingredients varies significantly depending on the density factor, e.g. 1 cup flour weighs less than 1 cup butter. Quantities in ingredients have been rounded up or down for convenience, where appropriate. Metric conversions may therefore not correspond exactly. It is important to use either American or metric measurements within a recipe.

British Cookery Terms

US	UK	US	UK
arugula	rocket salad	molasses	treacle
bacon slices	streaky bacon, streaky rashers	offal	variety meats
beet	beetroot	papaya	pawpaw
bouillon cube	stock cube	parsley root	Hamburg parsley
broil, broiler	grill, oven grill	peanut, peanut oil	groundnut, groundnut oil
chicory	endive	pit	stone (of fruits)
cilantro	fresh coriander leaves	porcini mushrooms	ceps, boletus or penny bun
coconut, shredded or grated	desiccated coconut	powdered sugar	icing sugar
cookie	biscuit (sweet)	rise	prove
corn	maize, sweetcorn	rutabaga	Swede
cornstarch	cornflour	seed	pip
eggplant	aubergine	shrimp	prawn
flour, all-purpose	plain flour	silvered almonds	flaked almonds
French fries	chips	snow peas, sugar peas	mangetout
golden raisins	sultanas	Swiss chard	chard
grill	barbecue	tart	flan
ground beef or pork	minced meat or mince	tofu	beancurd
ham (cured)	gammon	tomato paste	tomato puree
heavy (whipping) cream	double cream	whole wheat	wholemeal
jelly	jam	zucchini	courgette

© h.f.ullmann publishing GmbH
Original title: *Variationenkochbuch. Gemüse*
ISBN of the original edition: 978-3-8331-5866-7
Design, photography, layout, and typesetting: TLC Digitales Fotostudio GmbH & Co KG, Velen-Ramsdorf
Editors: Bettina Snowdon, Sylvia Winnewisser
Copy editing: Annerose Sieck

© for this English edition:
h.f.ullmann publishing GmbH

Translation from German: Mo Croasdale in association with First Edition Translations Ltd, Cambridge, UK
Editing: Sally Heavens in association with First Edition Translations Ltd, Cambridge, UK
Typesetting: Rob Partington in association with First Edition Translations Ltd, Cambridge, UK
Cover design: Hubert Hepfinger
Overall responsibility for production: h.f.ullmann publishing GmbH, Potsdam, Germany

ISBN 978-3-8480-0012-8

Printed in China

10 9 8 7 6 5 4 3 2 1
X IX VIII VII VI V IV III II I

www.ullmann-publishing.com
newsletter@ullmann-publishing.com

VARIATIONS
COOKBOOK

VEGETABLES

More than 200 basic recipes and variations

h.f.ullmann

CONTENTS

INTRODUCTION

You'll be amazed by these fabulous recipes for crispy, fresh, vegetable dishes!

Not only are they innovative, but they also leave you lots of freedom for trying out your own ideas. As well as classic dishes, you'll discover a whole range of unusual variations.

Take your time as you look through the book; let the pictures be your inspiration, read the suggestions in the Introduction, and then choose your vegetable recipe, according to the season.

Good luck—and bon appétit!

ABOUT THIS BOOK

Why choose this book?

You know the feeling: you're at the local farmers' market, and all around you are stalls with brightly colored, beautifully displayed vegetables. Sun-ripened, red tomatoes; green beans; red, yellow, and green bell peppers; tender young spinach; sweet carrots, pumpkins, and squash... Every season has its own delights, from freshly picked asparagus and tender young kohlrabi, through sugar snap peas, to cabbages in hues ranging from white and green through red, blue, and purple. You'll quite possibly find that one or other type of vegetable is in season or on offer, so you won't be able to resist and will choose a good quantity of whatever takes your fancy.

But, when you get home, the question you are faced with is—how to cook your wonderful purchases? Boil them, or sauté them in a little butter? Serve with a creamy sauce, or perhaps au gratin, or maybe make some soup? It is difficult to know what to do. What's the best way to cook asparagus? How do you skin bell peppers or tomatoes? Why is it that Brussels sprouts are tastiest after a frost? And which sauces and dips go best with which vegetables?

Our repertoire of recipes can be quite limited, especially when we'd like to try something that we don't often make. That's when a good cookbook really comes into its own! Most offer one or, at best, two ways of preparing a particular dish, and if you're lucky there might also be a sauce recipe—but only one.

Advantages

This book is different. It starts where other cookbooks finish—with variations on the recipes.

So, it does not only give you one recipe for the preparation of, for example, fresh broccoli, green cabbage, spinach, or celery; it gives

you at least four, with and without meat, plus a wide selection of side dishes with potatoes, pasta, rice, or dumplings, which you can vary in any way you please.

We also include a selection of unusual, out-of-the-ordinary sauces and dips for most dishes, alongside the classic accompaniments. You will also find a range of valuable tips and information on the various ingredients. You could say the book

provides a set of building blocks for innovative cooks.

How to use it

And this is how it goes: the book is divided into four chapters, one for each season of the year. There is usually one classic, basic recipe for each dish, which you might well have been wanting to know more about for a long time. And now these step by step instructions and detailed photographs will help you do just that. You will also find that the basic recipe page contains information on one of the ingredients, a particular method of preparation, or a recipe for a sauce or side dish.

The following double page spread has between four and six variations on the vegetable recipe, each with a highly informative photo. And, as a little bonus, we also provide you with other side dishes, such as potato purée, rice, pasta, polenta, and couscous—or delicious sauces that you can vary in accordance with your own ideas.

The recipes have been compiled to suit all tastes, and are taken from cuisines around the world. So, armed with this book, you can now create a vegetable dish for family and friends that will delight even the most exacting connoisseur!

No prior knowledge required

You do not require any prior knowledge in order to follow these recipes. What you do need is enthusiasm and a love of cooking—and all the usual kitchen equipment. Thanks to the descriptions and step by step instructions, even beginners will be able to prepare these dishes with ease.

And more experienced chefs will undoubtedly find many new ideas to put into practice. Plus, when there is a need to take particular care,

perhaps in the preparation of a particular vegetable, we make sure you are aware of it, so nothing should go wrong.

Variations

Light, easy, and very tasty—vegetables are talented all-rounders that, thanks to our varied and diverse recipes, can be prepared in lots of different ways, month after month.

You will find the best variations on each method for preparing the vegetables, to give you the widest possible selection to choose from. For some, we suggest a basic method according to the vegetable type, which we then vary with sauces or other ingredients. For others, we

suggest a main recipe and then give four or six separate variations that present the vegetable in the most diverse ways. Some variations can, in our opinion, only be combined with certain side dishes, sauces, and dips. Wherever this is the case, we point it out. But of course you are free to try out your own new taste experiences.

Vegetable quality

A word about quality. Carrots, spinach, etc. that are grown outdoors and without added chemicals are undeniably healthier and better digested than vegetables that are forced in glasshouses, given chemical fertilizers, and/or sprayed with preservatives—to say nothing of genetically modified vegetables, which you would do well to avoid at all costs.

We suggest you always make use of the vegetables that are in season and available in your local market or store. If you are fortunate enough to have your own vegetable garden, then you do not need to worry about the quality of your produce.

INFO
ORGANIC VEGETABLES

If you buy organic vegetables, you can be sure that no harmful substances will have been absorbed through the soil or the skin. Nor has anything been flown halfway around the world, which is good news for the environment as well. Today, most supermarkets and greengrocers have a range of organic produce on their shelves. You can taste the difference, too. Organic vegetables really do taste better, which has to be worth their slightly higher cost.

PREPARATION

Preparation

For reasons of space, we have omitted the basic instructions that always apply, unless otherwise stated. For instance, onions and garlic are always peeled before use, and potatoes and carrots are either scraped or peeled. Mushrooms should be wiped clean rather than washed, as they can absorb a lot of water. Chard, leeks, and spinach must be washed thoroughly, and white asparagus has to be peeled and the

Freshly harvested

Carrots, beans, and peas should be firm and crisp; leafy vegetables should have firm, juicy leaves; and asparagus stalks should "squeak" when rubbed together. Broccoli should have strong green leaves and florets; cauliflowers must not be bruised; and the skins of eggplant should be shiny and firm—as should bell peppers and tomatoes. The heads of mushrooms should be firm, with the gills closed. When buying

Kitchen equipment

It is not necessary to have a professional kitchen for these recipes. Of course, you should have a standard domestic stove top and oven, whether gas or electric, ceramic or induction.

wooden ends trimmed. Tomatoes, zucchini, and eggplant need to be "topped and tailed," and the cores of cabbages and chicory cut out. Vegetables with peel should be washed thoroughly first, as should salads and fresh herbs such as parsley, dill, and basil.

Incidentally, the water used for cooking vegetables can be used to make sauces or gravy if the vegetables are organic.

vegetables, always make sure that they are absolutely fresh. Use all your senses. The cut sections are important. They should still be moist, indicating that the vegetables were harvested earlier in the day.

In the case of vegetables such as zucchini and kohlrabi, it is worth buying small ones, as the larger ones are often fibrous and bland.

Lots of vegetables taste best when still firm to the bite (al dente), and only need cooking briefly. A wok—a flat-bottomed, circular, deep pan, much used in Asia—is ideal for this. Although a wok can be used for flash-frying, blanching, deep-frying, and steaming, the main method for cooking in a wok is stir-frying. The ingredients are simply cut into small pieces and cooked quickly in very hot oil. The wok is a healthy, low-energy cooking method; the vegetables stay crisp, their nutrients are preserved,

and the high sides of the wok prevent oil splashes.

Kitchen utensils

Vegetables can also be cooked healthily along with other ingredients such as meat or fish in a traditional clay cooker (it has to be soaked in

water before it goes in the oven) or in a steamer. Steaming is generally seen as the epitome of a healthy diet: full of vitamins, low in salt and

fat—and yet full of flavor.

The flavor, however, should be complemented with fresh herbs and a little oil. Rice lovers would do well to invest in a special rice cooker. It is very useful, because the rice is cooked perfectly.

INFO QUANTITIES

In this book you will find that the ingredients are always given in Imperial (American) measurements followed by the Metric equivalent. Please see page 2 for a conversion table and an explanation of the abbreviations.

For the recipes in this book, you will need at least 1 small, 1 medium, and 1 large pan; a tall pot for asparagus (ideally, an asparagus steamer); 1 large or several small gratin dishes and soufflé molds; and a casserole or roasting pan to hold either a joint, duck, goose, or chicken that is large enough for 4 people. Those who like light Asian cuisine will enjoy using a

wok. One or two skillets are best, ideally cast (aluminum or iron) with a non-scratch finish, plus 1 small pan for melting butter. A sieve for sifting and draining is indispensable, and a food mill for grinding ingredients for sauces etc., is also very useful.

Sharp knives are essential: large ones for chopping vegetables, and smaller ones for peeling and dicing fruit, for

example. A vegetable peeler is also a good idea, plus an asparagus peeler, and a serrated or rocking knife for onions, garlic, and herbs; a vegetable slicer or mandoline for thinly slicing cucumber and making julienne

(matchstick-shape) carrots, for example, and a grater for vegetables and cheese. It is also a good idea to have a nutmeg grater.

You should also ideally have 1 or 2 chopping boards made of wood or plastic to protect your work surfaces. Other useful kitchen tools include a potato ricer, a rolling pin, a slotted spoon, wooden spoons, a whisk, measuring cups and/or spoons,

bowls of various sizes made of metal and plastic, and kitchen scales. A food processor, blender, and electric handheld blender are also extremely useful for chopping and puréeing.

COOKING METHODS

Blanching

Vegetables are blanched by placing them in boiling water for a few minutes, then plunging them into ice water to halt the cooking process and to preserve the color. Blanched vegetables are typically used in gratins or stuffed dishes, e.g.

cabbage leaves. Vegetables with a short cooking time, such as spinach, chard, and sugar snap peas, are ideal for blanching. Mushrooms must not be blanched.

Poaching and glazing

Poached vegetables are cooked in a little liquid such as bouillon, stock, water, wine, or a tiny amount of oil.

Poaching is one of the gentlest and healthiest cooking methods. Glazing is a very special cooking method. It is ideal for carrots with a high starch content, and for onions and bolete. Glazing leaves the vegetables with a lovely glossy finish and rich color, since a little sugar is added to the cooking liquid.

Steaming

Steaming is even gentler than poaching. The vegetables do not come into contact with the water,

which means that none of their important nutrients leach into the cooking liquid. The vegetables are cooked in the water vapor (steam), which takes about 10–15 minutes, depending on the type of vegetable. This method retains the maximum color, structure, and flavor, as well as all goodness. It is suitable for all types of vegetable, especially those with a delicate flavor, such as asparagus.

Boiling

Depending on their type, the vegetables are cooked in boiling stock or salt water until soft, or just al dente. All vegetables can be

cooked this way—indeed some, such as green beans, have to be cooked, as they are toxic if consumed raw.

Frying and stewing

If the vegetables are to be fried in hot oil, the cooking time should be short. Some of the vegetables that benefit from this cooking method are bell peppers, zucchini, artichokes, fennel, mushrooms, and eggplant. If firmer vegetables, e.g. potatoes, are to be fried, they should be blanched beforehand. When stewed, the vegetables are first sweated in a little oil (i.e. cooked over low heat until they are soft, but not brown.) Cooking liquid is then added (water, bouillon, wine, etc.) and the vegetables are simmered over low heat until done.

Stir-frying

The preferred cooking utensil for this method is the wok. Chopped

vegetables are sautéed in hot oil: they are stirred continuously, for 2–3 minutes, then pushed to the side to drain. Any kind of vegetable can be stir-fried. Some very firm types should be blanched first.

Gratinate

Dishes served au gratin have a topping added at the final stage of cooking, in order to give them a

cheesy crust. Vegetable dishes with or without meat, poultry, or fish, or those that feature stuffed vegetables—most are suitable for serving au gratin. The crust consists of cheese and breadcrumbs, herbs, spices, and/or nuts. Gratination is done by placing the dish either in the oven, or under a hot broiler for a few minutes. The cheese melts and the topping turns a wonderful, golden-brown color.

Baking

Vegetables such as parsnips and potatoes can be roasted in the oven, but it is usual to blanch them first.

Potatoes baked in their skins do not require pre-cooking, but must be well scrubbed under running water beforehand. Eggplant or bell peppers

that need to be peeled should be baked first; this makes their skin blister, and therefore much easier to remove.

Grilling and broiling

Vegetables are ideal for grilling. You can either put them directly on the grill rack, or in a special container for barbecuing. An even gentler method is to wrap them in aluminum foil with a little herb butter, and then put them on the rack. Out of

barbecue season, you can cook vegetables in a stove-top grill, to give them the typical "grill stripes." The flavor, however, does not really compare with the smoky taste of "properly" barbecued vegetables. Corn on the cob, zucchini, bell peppers, eggplant, tomatoes, asparagus, salsify, and mushrooms are all ideal for grilling or broiling. In both cases, the vegetables should be brushed generously with a marinade or oil both before and during cooking, to prevent them from drying out.

Deep frying

Lots of vegetables can be deep fried until crispy, if they are first coated in a batter of some kind. The vegetables remain crisp and juicy, and the batter gives them a delicious crunch.

13

Sauces and dips

We recommend sauces and dips with lots of our dishes and variations. As we are limiting ourselves to stating the ingredients only, you should ideally have some cooking experience. Here are a few tips on making a sauce: save the vegetable juices after cooking, and mix them with water, bouillon, or wine to make a sauce that can then be finished with light cream, sour cream, yogurt, crème fraîche, or heavy cream. You can also add chopped herbs and spices for a piquant or fresh flavor. A horseradish or mustard sauce can also be made, to accompany boiled or steamed vegetables. This is based on a light

roux, for which flour is stirred into butter, then thinned with stock, and finished with the actual flavoring—mustard, horseradish, lemon juice, etc.

If you want to grill or broil vegetables and serve them with a dip, it is a good idea to make one with mayonnaise or quark.

The key factor is what you use to finish the dip—onions, stewed vegetables, mushrooms, meat or sausage, cheese, etc. There are also several ways to bind a sauce. The traditional method is with corn-starch, which is first stirred into a little water, and then added to the sauce. Flour and butter can also be

used: combine equal amounts and add very gradually to the bubbling sauce.

If vegetable pieces, potatoes, or fruit are being cooked in the sauce, they can be puréed when cooked to thicken it. Reducing the sauce takes a little longer. This gives the best result, however, as the taste and aroma of the ingredients become

concentrated as the sauce is reduced. A tomato sauce that reduces over several hours has a particularly intense flavor.

Reduced sauces can be made creamy by adding flakes of ice-cold butter. Whisk the butter into the sauce, and serve immediately—before the butter and sauce have the chance to separate. To thicken, stir egg yolk into a little milk or cream until smooth, and then pour slowly into the hot sauce. Important: the sauce must not be allowed to boil, or the

egg yolk will separate. When it comes to choosing your ingredients, there is no limit to what you can do. Unusual sauce ingredients such as Fanta®, Coca-Cola®, coffee, or melted chocolate also have their charms. Added in the right quantities, they can give your sauces a real kick!

Experiment to your heart's content, and discover the combinations that taste best to you!

Side dishes

We have tried to balance the side dishes. You will find potatoes in many different guises—from potato purée, fried potatoes, and dumplings through au gratin; rice in lots of variations—with vegetables, or with herbs and spices, or with fruit; and pasta, from fusilli through tagliatelle. But we have also included grain-based dishes, such and for rice, semolina, bulgur, and couscous, $1^1/_4$ cups (250 g). All these amounts are for 4 people. Experiment, and see whether you prefer to finish the rice, couscous, or bulgur with 1 or 2 onions, 2 or 3 bell peppers, $3^1/_2$ or $5^1/_2$ oz (100 or 150 g) of mushrooms, or to mix the polenta with 5 or 7 tablespoons grated Parmesan.

as polenta, bulgur, and couscous.

Again, we have not given any quantities, because we want the side dishes to be seen as suggestions only.

If we do not think that a particular side dish is right, perhaps because it would mask the delicate flavor of the vegetable, we include a suggestion for bread or croutons instead. Other additions are, of course, all kinds of meat, fish, and poultry: whether fried, stewed, steamed, broiled, grilled, or served au gratin. Here too, you can give in entirely to your own taste!

A tip: for potatoes, base your quantities on about $1^3/_4$–$2^1/_4$ lb (800 g–1 kg); for pasta, 14 oz (400 g);

Herbs and spices

Herbs and spices are the dot on the "i" of every dish. Their flavors emphasize or complement those of vegetables, and they also have various health benefits. Many of them stimulate the digestive system. As a general rule, fresher means better. Herbs popular with chefs include parsley, chives, dill, fennel, chervil, tarragon, lovage, marjoram, thyme, oregano, sage, cilantro, and basil.

Fresh herbs are finely chopped, and most first have the leaves removed from their stalks. The exception to this is chives, as it is the stem of this herb that is used.

Of course, dried herbs are always an option.

Spices and seasonings can be bought ready ground, but this is often at the cost of taste. If at all possible, freshly grind or grate your salt, pepper, and nutmeg.

VITAMIN CHART

This seasonal chart shows you at a glance which essential vitamins are present in the various vegetables. In the list of vitamin RDAs, the first figure is based on the daily requirement for women, the second on that for men. The values are based on 3¹/₂ oz (100 g) of the fresh product.

Spring	A (retinol)	B 1 (thiamine)	B 2 (ribo-flavin)	B 6 (pyri-doxine)	C (ascorbic acid)	D (calciferol)	E (toco-pherol)
Asparagus	0	0.11	0.1	0.06	20	0	0
Potatoes	0	0.08	0.04	0.21	12.04	0	0.05
Leaf spinach	0	0.11	0.23	0.22	52	0	1.36
Sugar snap peas	0	0.17	0.15	0.16	25	0	0.5
Chard	0	0.09	0.16	0.09	39	0	1.5
Cauliflower	0	0.11	0.1	0.2	73	0	0.08
Kohlrabi	0	0.04	0.04	0.12	64	0	0.4
Mushrooms	0.03	0.08	0.35	0.05	4.31	1.61	0.21

Summer	A (retinol)	B 1 (thiamine)	B 2 (ribo-flavin)	B 6 (pyri-doxine)	C (ascorbic acid)	D (calciferol)	E (toco-pherol)
Broccoli	0	0.09	0.172	0.17	115	0	0.62
Celery stalks	0	0.04	0.07	0.09	7	0	0.2
Fava beans	0	0.22	0.14	0.2	33	0	0.3
Zucchini	0	0.07	0.09	0.08	16	0	0.5
Bell peppers, green	0	0.05	0.4	0.27	139	0	2.5
Green beans	0	0.08	0.12	0.28	20	0	0.13
Tomatoes	0	0.05	0.03	0.1	24.5	0	0.81
Fennel	0	0.23	0.11	0.1	93	0	6
Carrots	1700	0.1	0.05	0.6	7	0	0.5

Vitamins	A (retinol)	B 1 (thiamine)	B 2 (ribo-flavin)	B 6 (pyri-doxine)	C (ascorbic acid)	D (calciferol)	E (toco-pherol)
RDA	0.8–1 mg	1–1.3 mg	1.2–1.5 mg	1.2–1.6 mg	60–100-mg	0.005 mg	12–15 mg

Fall	A (retinol)	B 1 (thiamine)	B 2 (ribo-flavin)	B 6 (pyri-doxine)	C (ascorbic acid)	D (calciferol)	E (toco-pherol)
Leeks	0	0.08	0.06	0.25	24	0	0.5
Corn	0	0.26	0.3	0.4	0	0	2.1
Celeriac	0	0.03	0.07	0.2	8.25	0	0.53
Beet	2	0.01	0.02	0.05	10	0	0.05
Pumpkin/squash	0	0.09	0.06	0.15	14	0	0.1
Chanterelles	0.01	0.03	0.15	0.04	4.35	1.52	0.57
Eggplant	0	0.03	0.04	0.08	5	0	0.03
Sweetheart cabbage	0	0.06	0.06	0.15	60	0	0.15
Salsify	0	0.11	0.03	0.07	4	0	6

Winter	A (retinol)	B 1 (thiamine)	B 2 (ribo-flavin)	B 6 (pyri-doxine)	C (ascorbic acid)	D (calciferol)	E (toco-pherol)
Savoy cabbage	0	0.06	0.05	2	49.4	0	2.5
White cabbage	0	0.04	0.03	0.11	45.8	0	1.7
Sauerkraut	0	0.02	0.0	0.21	20	0	0.15
Chicory	0	0.05	0.03	0.05	8.68	0	0.1
Brussels sprouts	0	0.12	0.13	0.28	112	0	0.56
Red cabbage	0	0.06	0.05	0.15	50	0	1.7
Kale	0	0.1	0.25	0.25	125	0	1.7

Vitamins B, C and E in mg/100 g; vitamins A and D in μ/100 g (1 μ = 1/1000 mg).

SPRING

Spring has come!

Once again, fresh vegetables are available—starting with fabulous green and white asparagus in May.

Tender young spinach is also available to enrich the menu.

These delights will soon be followed by sweet sugar snap peas, kohlrabi, cauliflower, and Swiss chard.

This chapter contains a range of recipes for these fresh vegetables, side dishes, and sauces.

ASPARAGUS
with ham and butter

INFO

Unlike white asparagus, green asparagus has had plenty of light before being harvested, which is what gives it its green color. The skin is not as hard as that of white asparagus, so only the lower third needs to be peeled. Depending on the thickness of the stalks, it will also require less cooking time.

Serves 4

2 kg	*white asparagus, stalks of equal size*
	Salt
	Sugar
7 tbsp (100 g)	*butter*
7 oz (200 g)	*boiled or cured ham, sliced*

Step by step

Thinly peel the asparagus with a vegetable peeler (making sure to leave the tips intact). Cut off the dry and woody ends.

Bring some water to a boil in a tall asparagus pot with salt, a pinch of sugar, and 1 tablespoon of butter.

Cook the asparagus al dente for about 15–20 minutes, depending on the thickness.

Heat the remainder of the butter in a small pan and pour into a gravy boat.

Roll the asparagus stalks in individual slices of ham, arrange on plates, and serve with the melted butter.

Side dish

Asparagus is traditionally served with **new potatoes**. If you are lucky, you might be able to find some in May—the wonderful aroma harmonizes perfectly with that of the asparagus. There is no need to peel the potatoes, as the skin will still be thin and tender with a delicate aroma. Scrub $1^3/_4$ lb (750 g) new potatoes well under running water then cook in their skins for about 20 minutes. You could also serve a portion of scrambled eggs with asparagus and ham.

Sauce

Either serve the asparagus just with melted butter, which perfectly complements the flavor of these wonderful stalks, or with a basic, light, homemade **hollandaise**: stir together 1 teaspoon cornstarch with 1 cup (250 ml) bouillon and 2 tablespoons lemon juice. Whisk in a bain marie until creamy. Gradually beat in $3^1/_2$ tablespoons (50 g) flaked butter. Season with salt, pepper, sugar, and 2 tablespoons light cream.

ASPARAGUS
several variations

Back again at the end of April, sometimes a little sooner: fresh asparagus, both white and green. Make the most of it while it's available, because the season ends on June 24, St. John's Day.

... au gratin with cured ham and egg cream

Arrange 4$^1/_2$ lb (2 kg) asparagus and 7 oz (200 g) cured ham, cut into strips, in an ovenproof dish. Beat together 3 eggs, $^1/_2$ cup (125 ml) light cream, 2 tablespoons melted butter, 3 tablespoons grated Gouda, and salt, and pour over the asparagus. Sprinkle over 4$^1/_2$ oz (125 g) chopped ham, and bake at 400 °F/200 °C. for 10 minutes. Garnish with 1 tablespoon chopped dill and 2 chopped tomatoes.

... with soy sauce and ginger

Peel the lower one-third of 2$^1/_4$ lb (1 kg) green asparagus. Sauté lightly in a little oil. Mix together 4 tablespoons soy sauce, a little Worcestershire sauce, and 2 tablespoons finely grated ginger, and add to the asparagus. Cover with a lid and cook. The asparagus should still be al dente. Season with a little sesame oil.

... with a buttered Parmesan crust

Peel the lower one-third of 2$^1/_4$ lbs (1 kg) green asparagus and cook for about 8 minutes, so it is still al dente, and arrange in an ovenproof dish. Mix 3$^1/_2$ oz (100 g) grated Parmesan with fresh breadcrumbs made from 4 slices white bread, crusts removed, and sprinkle over the asparagus. Pour over 6 oz (180 g) melted butter. Bake at 400 °F–425 °F/200 °C–220 °C for 15 minutes.

.... with a filbert crust

Mix generous 1 lb (500 g) finely chopped filberts with 7 oz (200 g) dried bread crumbs. Dip 4$^1/_2$ lb (2 kg) cooked asparagus in a little flour, then in 2 beaten eggs, and finally in the nut mixture. Press the mixture firmly onto the asparagus. Sauté in plenty of oil or clarified butter until golden brown and season with salt, coriander, and tandoori spice.

... with salmon, potatoes, and a cheese crust

Cut 1¹/₄ lb (600 g) salmon fillets into strips, simmer in 3 table-spoons each vegetable bouillon and white wine, then drain. Place in an ovenproof dish with 1³/₄ lb (800 g) each cooked asparagus, cut into chunks, and sliced, boiled potatoes. Sprinkle with 4 table-spoons chopped chervil. Mix 7 oz (200 g) grated pecorino, 1 egg, generous ³/₄ cup (200 ml) crème fraîche, and salt. Pour over the salmon and vegetables and bake at 400 °F/200 °C for 10 minutes.

... with bell peppers and sesame

Peel 2¹/₄ lb (1 kg) green asparagus. Blanch for 5 minutes then cut into small pieces. Sauté 2 red bell peppers, cut into strips, with 1 chopped garlic clove and 1 sliced, deseeded chile for about 1 minute. Add the asparagus pieces and sauté for 2 minutes. Sprinkle over 2 tbsp each soy sauce and sesame oil, and coat the asparagus. Scatter over 2 tablespoons toasted sesame seeds.

SAUCES
for asparagus

If the traditional hollandaise is too boring for you, then why not pep it up a little!

Tarragon hollandaise

Whisk together an egg yolk and yogurt, ¹/₂ bunch chopped tarragon, and salt. Add the melted butter, first in drops, and then in a thin trickle. Goes well with asparagus and ham, mushrooms, and peas.

Filbert hollandaise

Whisk together an egg yolk, yogurt, ground filberts, and salt. Add the melted butter, first in drops, and then in a thin trickle. Garnish with orange zest.

Bell pepper hollandaise

Bake red bell peppers in the oven until the skin starts to blister. Remove the skin and seeds, then purée with ancho-vies, garlic, and ground almonds. Stir into the hollandaise instead of lemon juice. Season with salt and pepper.

POTATOES
INFO

Potatoes are starchy tubers and a member of the nightshade family; they come in an astonishing number of varieties (over 5,000). Today, they are grown in 130 countries. The tubers come as early potatoes, available from the

middle of May, medium early potatoes from August, and late varieties, which are harvested from mid-September through November. There are waxy varieties, the best known of which are Red Rose, White Rose, and Yukon Gold, through mealy varieties, such as Idaho and russet. Waxy potatoes retain their firm texture and smooth skin during cooking. They are suitable for sautéing, salads, casseroles, and gratins. Small, waxy new potatoes are delicious when cooked and eaten in their skins. Moderately waxy potatoes remain quite firm after cooking. They should be peeled, and are suitable for boiling, French fries, rösti, and potato cakes. Mealy potatoes have the highest starch content. They burst easily while cooking, and may even collapse entirely. They are, however, excellent at absorbing liquids, which makes them perfect for mashing, dumplings, soups, and stews.

Serves 4

2¹/₄ lb (1 kg)	*waxy new potatoes*
	Salt
1 tsp	*cumin*
generous 1 lb (500 g)	*quark*
7 tbsp (100 ml)	*light cream*
7 tbsp (100 ml)	*milk*
1 bunch	*parsley, chopped*
1 bunch	*chives, chopped*
¹/₂ bunch	*chervil, chopped*
2	*scallions, cut into rings*
	Pepper
3 tbsp	*linseed oil*

Step by step

Thoroughly wash the potatoes then boil in water with salt and cumin for 20 minutes.

Pour the linseed oil over the quark.

Stir the quark, cream, and milk together until smooth.

Drain the potatoes and leave to steam.

Add the herbs and scallions to the quark mixture, and season with salt and pepper.

Peel the potatoes if desired, and serve with the quark dressing.

NEW POTATOES
with herb quark and linseed oil

DIPS
for new potatoes

Try these dips instead of quark to go with new potatoes or their variations.

Chervil cream
Stir together 1 bunch of chopped chervil, crème fraîche, yogurt, curry powder, ground paprika, and salt. Goes well with potatoes boiled in their skins.

Mojo verde
Purée a garlic clove, green bell peppers, ground cumin, and olive oil. Add chopped parsley and season to taste with salt, pepper, and vinegar. Goes well with all versions.

Basil and cream cheese dip
Combine basil strips, finely chopped scallions, goat's cheese, 3 tablespoons sherry, salt, and pepper. Goes well with all versions.

NEW POTATOES
several

Nothing is more delicious than new potatoes dotted with a little butter and served with a refreshing dip or dressing. This enables their flavor thoroughly to penetrate the taste buds. A crisp salad also perfectly complements the potato experience. There are,

... au gratin with sesame
Thoroughly wash $1^3/_4$ lb (800 g) small, waxy new potatoes, cook in boiling salt water for 15 minutes, and drain. Halve the potatoes. Stir together 4 teaspoons toasted sesame seeds with 1 teaspoon coarse salt, $^2/_3$ cup (75 g) freshly grated Gruyère, a little black pepper, and 4 tablespoons crème fraîche. Brush over the potato halves, then place on a greased baking sheet and bake at 400 °F/200 °C.

... au gratin with spring vegetables
Slice generous 1 lb (500 g) cooked potatoes, and sprinkle with salt. Cook 9 oz (250 g) asparagus pieces until al dente. Cut 7 oz (200 g) kohlrabi into sticks, slice 7 oz (200 g) carrots, and cook with 7 oz (200 g) sugar snap peas until al dente. Place the potatoes and vegetables in a greased gratin dish and drizzle with 4 tablespoons bouillon. Sprinkle with a mixture of 11 oz (300 g) grated Gouda and 3 tablespoons dried breadcrumbs. Bake at 400 °F/200 °C for 30 minutes.

variations

however, other ways of preparing them as well. Our variations show four options: as a gratin with spring vegetables, stuffed with tasty wild garlic butter, topped with sesame, and as a typical "rheinische Ädappeltaat." Enjoy!

... as "Rheinische Ädappeltaat"

Grate 3 ¹/₄ lb (1.5 kg) potatoes and 3 onions. Dust with 1 table-spoon flour and leave to stand for a while. Drain well, retaining the starchy juices. Return them to the mixture. Stir 4 eggs into the potato mixture, and season with salt and pepper. Pour 4 table-spoons oil into a gratin dish. Line the bottom with 6 oz (175 g) bacon rashers then spread over the potato mixture. Sprinkle with oil, and bake at 430 °F/225 °C for 1 hour. Turn out onto a plate.

... as stuffed potatoes with wild garlic butter

Combine 7 tablespoons (100 g) butter with 2 tablespoons each wild garlic and parsley, and season with salt, pepper, and lemon juice. Chill. Dice 1 yellow and 1 red bell pepper, and 7 oz (200 g) each tomatoes and zucchini. Sweat in 3 tablespoons butter. Halve 8 boiled potatoes, scoop out the insides, and chop. Combine with the vegetable mixture, 1 tablespoon butter, and 9 oz (250 g) diced cheese, and spoon back into the potatoes. Bake at 400 °F/200 °C for 15 minutes. Dot with the wild garlic butter to serve.

SALADS
for new potatoes

A salad of cucumber and wild herbs or a colorful mixed salad are perfect with potato dishes.

Cucumber salad with yogurt dressing

Salt a finely chopped cucumber, and allow the juices to drain. Mix the cucumber with yogurt, water, vinegar, oil, pepper, sugar, and chopped dill.

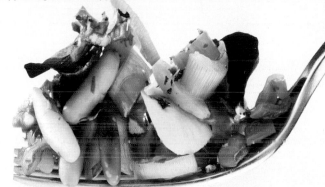

Wild herb salad

Combine chopped wild herbs with parsley, basil, and edible flowers. Sauté scallions and pine nuts, season with salt, pepper, and sugar, and scatter over the top.

Mixed leaf salad with peaches

Combine mixed salad leaves with arugula, strips of cured ham, and canned peaches. Drizzle with a dressing of oil, vinegar, salt, pepper, and chopped nuts.

LEAF SPINACH
with crème fraîche and Parmesan

INFO

Is it safe to reheat **spinach**? Yes—it's no longer a problem. Providing, of course, that it is kept chilled after cooking. This largely (if not completely) prevents the nitrate in it from changing into the more harmful type. So put cooked spinach in the icebox, and you can safely enjoy it the next day.

Serves 4

2¹/₄ lb (1 kg)	*leaf spinach, washed*
	Salt
3 tsp	*butter*
3 tbsp	*flour*
2 cups (500 ml)	*milk*
1	*shallot, finely chopped*
3 tbsp	*Parmesan, grated*
2 tbsp	*crème fraîche*
	Pepper
	Nutmeg

Step by step

Blanch the spinach in boiling salt water for 2 minutes. Remove and drain thoroughly.

Allow the spinach to cool slightly. Squeeze to remove the remaining water, then chop coarsely.

Melt the butter in a small pan. Add the flour, stirring continuously.

Add the milk and shallot, and bring to a boil. Simmer, stirring continuously, for 1 to 2 minutes until thickened.

Stir in the Parmesan and crème fraîche and season with pepper and nutmeg. Fold the spinach into the sauce.

Side dish

Potatoes in their skins are traditionally served with creamed spinach—the easiest way to prepare potatoes. This is how it's done: scrub 1³/₄ lb (750 g) waxy potatoes thoroughly under running water. Boil in plenty of salt water for about 20 minutes, then drain and serve. Do not forget to provide everyone with a peeling knife.

Side dish

A **fried egg** is essential with creamed spinach! And, in fact, cooking the perfect fried egg is also a skill that requires some practice. Melt 2 tablespoons butter in a skillet over medium heat. Crack in 4 eggs and allow them to glide around the skillet. Cook over low heat. Tilt the skillet slightly so they don't stick. When the egg whites set and turn white, sprinkle salt and pepper over the edges. The yolk should remain soft, and is not salted. For eggs sunny-side-up, spoon a little of the cooking fat over the yolk so the outer layer sets, or flip the eggs over if you prefer a firm yolk.

MEAT
with spinach

Spinach is also, of course, an excellent ingredient for sauces served with pasta, meat, or fish.

Duck breast

Fry 4 duck breasts in hot oil, skin side first, for 6 minutes. Turn over and continue cooking for 2 minutes. Wrap in aluminum foil and bake in the oven at 400 °F/200 °C for 15 minutes. Turn off the oven and leave to rest for 5 minutes.

... au gratin with Emmental

Wilt $2^1/_4$ lb (1 kg) spinach in 2 cups (500 ml) bouillon. Layer a third of the spinach in a dish, top with scant 1 cup (100 g) grated Emmental, 2 tablespoons chopped parsley, and a little thyme, and season with salt, pepper, and lemon juice. Repeat twice. Finish by drizzling 3 tablespoons olive oil over the top, and bake at 440 °F/200 °C for 10–15 minutes.

Turkey roulade stuffed with ham and carrot

Season 4 thin turkey escalopes with salt and pepper. Roll into sausage shapes with a stuffing of chopped boiled ham and blanched julienne carrots. Fry for 10 minutes in hot oil.

... as dumplings in tomato sauce

Combine $2^1/_4$ lb (1 kg) blanched, chopped spinach, 3 crumbled bread rolls previously softened in milk, $5^1/_2$ oz (150 g) sweated, chopped shallot, 1 egg, 2 tablespoons all-purpose flour, salt, pepper, and nutmeg. Shape into 10 balls and simmer in boiling salt water for 10 minutes. In another pan, simmer 1 chopped and sweated garlic clove with 14 oz (400 g) canned tomatoes and $3^1/_2$ oz (100 g) pitted black olives and season with salt and pepper. Serve with Parmesan.

LEAF SPINACH
several variations

Spinach quickly shrinks, so don't be surprised if you find that what started out as over two pounds in weight reduces to less than a third!

... with herbs, for ravioli

Combine generous 1 lb (500 g) all-purpose flour with 2 eggs, salt, and 1 tablespoon oil. Fry 5¹/₂ oz (150 g) fresh breadcrumbs in butter until golden. Steam 3 tablespoons each parsley and sliced chives plus 9 oz (250 g) finely chopped spinach, and leave to cool. Combine with 2 eggs and scant 1 cup (100 g) grated Parmesan. Roll the ravioli dough out very thinly. Cut into squares, then top with a little filling and fold in half diagonally. Squeeze together, and cook for 5–7 minutes.

... as spinach lasagna

Sweat 2¹/₄ lb (1 kg) spinach with 1 chopped onion. Combine 1 cup (250 ml) bouillon, 7 oz (200 g) quark, and ²/₃ cup (150 ml) light cream, and season with salt, pepper, sweet chile, and 1 pinch nutmeg. Alternate layers of ready to cook lasagna sheets, spinach, sauce, and ²/₃ cup (75 g) grated Parmesan in a gratin dish. Finish with sauce and 3¹/₂ tablespoons (25 g) grated cheese. Bake at 400 °F/200 °C for about 30 minutes.

... with tomatoes and Feta in a quiche

Blanch and roughly chop 2¹/₄ lb (1 kg) spinach. Roll out 1 lb (450 g) puff pastry. Combine 2 chopped garlic cloves, 3¹/₂ oz (100 g) canned tomato passato, salt, and pepper and pour into the pastry shell. Top with 7 oz (200 g) diced boiled ham and the spinach. Mix together 1¹/₄ cups (300 ml) light cream, 4 eggs, salt, and oregano, and pour over. Sprinkle with 7 oz (200 g) diced Feta and bake at 400 °F/200 °C for 30 minutes.

... with ricotta, for wraps

Combine 2¹/₄ lb (1 kg) blanched, chopped spinach with 9 oz (250 g) ricotta, half the amount of 2 chopped, sautéed onions, and salt. Use to fill 4 soft, fried tortillas. Place in an ovenproof dish and top with 14 oz (400 g) canned tomatoes, salt, pepper, chile powder, basil, and the remainder of the onions. Bake at 480 °F/250 °C for 15 minutes, then sprinkle with 1¹/₄ cups (125 g) grated Parmesan and bake at 350 °F/175 °C for a further 10 minutes.

SUGAR SNAP PEAS
with almond butter

Serves 4

1 ¹/₄ lb (600 g)	sugar snap peas
	Salt
3 tbsp	butter
2 tbsp	chopped almonds
	Pepper

Step by step

Trim the sugar snap peas, and remove the threads. Wash and drain thoroughly.

Stir in the almonds and sauté until golden.

Simmer the sugar snap peas in boiling salt water for around 5 minutes. Strain.

Add the sugar snap peas and shake well to cover with the almond butter.

Melt the butter in a pan and brown a little.

Season with salt and pepper and serve immediately.

SUGAR SNAP PEAS INFO

There is more than one name for the **sugar snap pea**. Though it

looks more like a flattened bean, it is in fact a hybrid of the English pea and snow pea and also known as mangetout, French for "eat all," which tells us that we can indeed eat the whole pod when it is young. The tender pods are delicious raw; when steamed and buttered, they are an absolute delight.

ALMOND INFO

Almond trees belong to the rose family, and only thrive in a very mild climate. Originally from the Mediterranean, they are now more widely cultivated, including in California. We differentiate between bitter almonds, which we shouldn't eat, and sweet almonds.

Amygdalin, a component of which is hydrocyanic (prussic) acid, is the substance present in both varieties, giving them their unmistakable flavor. Bitter almond oil is a basic ingredient of marzipan.

SUGAR SNAP PEAS
several variations

Sugar snap peas can be steamed or sautéed; both options are delicious. They are also a popular ingredient in Asian cuisine. Their short cooking time makes them ideal for frying in a wok.

... with garlic and sesame

Sauté 2 sliced garlic cloves in 4 tablespoons oil until golden, then remove from the oil. Fry 1¹/₄ lb (600 g) sugar snap peas briefly in 1 tablespoon of the garlic oil. Return the garlic and deglaze the pan with 3 tablespoons soy sauce. Season with pepper, sugar, and 3 teaspoons toasted sesame seeds.

... with cilantro and lime juice

Blanch 1¹/₄ lb (600 g) sugar snap peas in boiling salt water for about 5 minutes. Melt 2 tablespoons butter in a skillet and season with 1 teaspoon lime juice, ¹/₂ bunch chopped cilantro, salt, and pepper. Fry the sugar snap peas briefly in the butter, and serve hot.

... with eggplant, tomatoes, and pesto

Dice 1 eggplant and 1 zucchini, and halve 5¹/₂ oz (150 g) sugar snap peas. Fry over medium heat in 4 tablespoons olive oil. When the vegetables are soft, add 9 oz (250 g) cherry tomatoes and 2 tablespoons pesto, then season with salt and pepper. Simmer for a further 4 minutes.

... with duck breast and orange

Remove the skins from 2 fat duck breasts. Fry in a hot skillet till the fat runs, then remove. Cut the duck breast into strips, sauté over high heat, and season with salt and pepper. Deglaze the pan with 1 teaspoon each balsamic vinegar and soy sauce. Add 1¹/₄ lb (600 g) sugar snap peas and cook briefly. Add the segments of 2 oranges and a little orange juice to the duck.

SIDE DISHES
for sugar snap peas

Rice makes the best accompaniment for dishes with sugar snap peas. Try the oriental versions: curry and cilantro rice, and lime rice.

Curry powder and cilantro rice

Sweat 1¹/₄ cups (250 g) long-grain rice in butter until transparent then pour over double the quantity of liquid. Season with salt and simmer gently over low heat for 20 minutes. Stir in flakes of butter and chopped cilantro.

Wholegrain wild rice mix

Sweat 1¹/₄ cups (250 g) wild rice mix in butter with some chopped onion. Pour over twice the amount of bouillon. Simmer gently over low heat for 40–45 minutes.

Lime rice

Cook 1¹/₄ cups (250 g) long-grain rice in twice the amount of water with salt and a bay leaf until al dente. Add finely chopped mint and the grated rind of a lime.

... with pork and ginger

Heat 4 tablespoons oil in a skillet and fry generous 1 lb (500 g) pork fillet strips for 1 minute, season with salt. Add 1 teaspoon freshly grated ginger and 1 chopped garlic clove then sauté over high heat for 1 minute. Add 1¹/₄ lb (600 g) sugar snap peas and continue frying for 2 minutes. Mix together 4 tablespoons each red wine vinegar, ketchup, and sugar, and bring to a boil.

... with Chinese mushrooms

Slice 8 soaked Chinese mushrooms and fry in 3 tablespoons oil in a wok with 4 sliced scallions, generous 1 lb (500 g) halved sugar snap peas, and 2 chopped garlic cloves. Mix together ²/₃ cup (150 ml) vegetable bouillon, 2 tablespoons soy sauce, a dash of fruit vinegar, and some honey, and pour into the wok. Bring to a boil and season to taste with salt, pepper, and cayenne.

CHARD
INFO

As a type of beet, **chard** is related to sugar beet and animal fodder. Varieties include Swiss chard, which is also called stem

chard because of its broad, flat stems, and thin-stemmed leaf chard, also known as perpetual spinach. Swiss chard is notable for the highly developed ribs on the leaves; they and the stems are edible. Only the leaves of leaf chard are used. Once cut, it grows new leaves that can also be harvested. Swiss chard is the longest lasting, and the variety usually found in stores. When cooking, remember that the stems need to cook for longer than the leaves. They are usually cut into smaller pieces and steamed separately with the thick center rib, the chopped leaves being added a few minutes later.

GRUYÈRE
INFO

Gruyère is a hard cheese made from raw cow's milk from the Greyerzerland. Tasty Gruyère, also called Greyerzer, has a somewhat grainy consistency with a nutty aroma. It melts very well, and is ideal for

gratins. It is traditionally used in a Swiss cheese fondue.

36

Serves 4	
2¼ lb (1 kg)	*Swiss chard*
1 tsp	*lemon juice*
2 tbsp	*butter*
1	*onion, finely chopped*
1 cup (250 ml)	*soured cream*
	Salt
	Pepper
	Nutmeg
1⅓ cups (150 g)	*Gruyère, grated*

Step by step

Remove the chard leaves from the stems, wash, and cut into very thin strips.

Add the chard leaves, and simmer for a further 5 minutes. Combine with the cream, salt, pepper, and nutmeg.

Wash the chard stems, trim the lower ends, and cut into 2-in. (5-cm) strips.

Arrange the mixture in a gratin dish. Sprinkle with the grated Gruyère.

Sprinkle the stems with lemon juice and cook in butter with chopped onions until al dente.

Bake in a preheated oven at 425 °F/220 °C for about 20 minutes.

SWISS CHARD
gratin with Gruyère

SWISS CHARD
several variations

You can use stem or leaf chard for these recipes. If using stem chard, remember that the stems need to be cooked for longer.

... rolled with a ground meat filling

Blanch 12 Swiss chard leaves—flatten the ribs—and cool. Combine 11 oz (300 g) ground meat with 1 egg, 1 chopped garlic clove, 1 softened bread roll, 3$\frac{1}{2}$ oz (100 g) Feta, and pepper. Spoon over the leaves and roll them up into sausage shapes. Simmer for 20 minutes in 4 tablespoons white wine, $\frac{1}{2}$ cup (125 ml) bouillon, and 2 tablespoons olive oil. Remove, then bring the cooking broth to a boil with 1/4 pint (150 g) canned passato and pour over.

... in flaky pastry parcels with fish

Roll out 1 lb (450 g) flaky pastry dough and place on a greased baking sheet. Remove the stalks from 8–12 Swiss chard leaves and cook, then drain and leave to cool. Season 14 oz (400 g) white fish with salt and pepper. Lay the chard leaves over the pastry, leaving an edge. Spread with 1 tablespoon creamed horseradish then top with the fish. Fold up and seal the pastry and brush with egg yolk. Bake at 350 °F/180 °C for 30 minutes.

... with a Roquefort and nut crust

Blanch the chopped stalks of 2$\frac{1}{4}$ lb (1 kg) Swiss chard for 8 minutes, adding the sliced leaves after 3 minutes. Drain, then place in a gratin dish. Crumble 5$\frac{1}{2}$ oz (150 g) Roquefort over the top. Stir a little yeast-based seasoning into $\frac{2}{3}$ cup (150 ml) light cream and pour over. Sprinkle with 2 tablespoons chopped nuts. Bake at 425 °F/220 °C for 15–20 minutes.

... with red lentils, ginger, and cumin

Sweat 2 chopped onions, 2 chopped garlic cloves, and 1 teaspoon freshly grated ginger in a little butter. Add 2 tablespoons sesame seeds, 1 teaspoon cumin, and $\frac{1}{2}$ teaspoon turmeric, and cook briefly. Add 9 oz (250 g) red lentils, 14 oz (400 g) Swiss chard—stalks diced, leaves cut into strips—1 cup (250 ml) coconut milk, 1 cup (250 ml) bouillon, and salt, and simmer for 15 minutes. Season to taste with lemon juice.

SIDE DISHES
for Swiss chard

Potato dishes go very well with Swiss chard, especially with added herbs.

Herby potatoes
Sauté cubed, raw potatoes and diced onions in oil until crisp. Add chopped herbs, salt, and pepper to taste. Goes well with the Roquefort and fava bean recipes.

Potatoes au gratin
Arrange slices of potato in an ovenproof dish. Season with salt, pepper, and nutmeg and sprinkle with grated Gouda. Mix together light cream, milk, and cheese and pour over, then bake at 400 °F/200 °C for 50–60 minutes. Goes well with the fava bean variation.

Potato purée
Boil some potatoes in their skins, then peel and push through a ricer. Combine with milk and butter, and season with salt and nutmeg. Goes well with the chard rolls.

... as salad, with mushrooms and croutons
Blanch 1³/₄ lb (800 g) Swiss chard leaves in boiling water. Drain, then cut into strips. Arrange on plates with 1³/₄ oz (50 g) thinly sliced mushrooms. Make a dressing from 1 chopped onion, 4 tablespoons wine vinegar, 6 tablespoons oil, sugar, salt, and pepper, and pour over. Scatter with 5 tablespoons grated mountain cheese and some butter-fried croutons.

... with fava beans, olives, and bacon
Fry 9 oz (250 g) diced bacon in a skillet until crisp, then remove. Sweat 11 oz (300 g) fava beans with 14 oz (400 g) diced Swiss chard and 1 chopped onion in olive oil. Add 1 cup (250 ml) vegetable bouillon and 3 tablespoons tomato paste and simmer gently for 10 minutes. Add 2 oz (60 g) pitted black olives and the bacon. Heat for 3 minutes. Season with salt, pepper, thyme, and 1 tablespoon lemon juice.

CAULIFLOWER
in cream sauce

Serves 4

1	large cauliflower (about 2¼ lb/1 kg
	Salt
3–4 tbsp	all-purpose flour
5–6 tbsp	butter
2 cups (500 ml)	vegetable bouillon
7 tbsp (100 ml)	light cream
	Pepper
	Nutmeg
1 tsp	lemon juice

INFO

In the nineteenth century, **cauliflower** was still considered one of the most sophisticated of all vegetables, together with artichokes and asparagus. Today, it is an integral part of daily cuisine, and is available almost all year round. The little florets are not naturally white, but are kept out of the sun by tying the green leaves together over the head of the cauliflower. This prevents chlorophyll from forming.

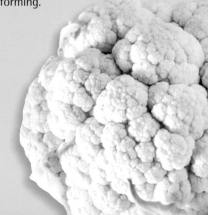

Step by step

Trim the cauliflower, removing the leaves and thick stalk, then cut off any brown parts and break into florets.

Bring some salted water to a boil in a large pan, and cook the cauliflower florets for about 15 minutes.

Remove from the water with a slotted spoon, then drain and set aside.

Make a roux with the flour in 3–4 tablespoons butter, and gradually add the vegetable bouillon.

Simmer gently for about 10 minutes, stirring frequently. Then pour in the cream and bring briefly to a boil.

Season with salt, pepper, nutmeg, and lemon juice, and stir in the remainder of the butter. Pour the sauce over the cauliflower.

INFO

There are lots of different ways of stuffing **tomatoes**. The traditional way is with ground meat. However, rice, bulgur, couscous, rice noodles, herbs, vegetables, cheese, or tofu can also all be used. It is important to hollow out the tomatoes, leaving about $1/2$ in. (1 cm) flesh. They should not disintegrate when they are cooked.

Side dish

Mashed potatoes: Peel $2^1/_4$ lb (1 kg) mealy potatoes, then halve and cook in boiling water for about 20 minutes. Meanwhile, peel and chop 1 onion and sweat in 1 tablespoon oil until transparent.

Add $1^3/_4$ oz (50 g) diced bacon and cook until crisp. Drain the potatoes, then mash and combine with the onion and bacon. Season with salt, pepper, and nutmeg.

SAUCES
for cauliflower

Cauliflower is delicious served with creamy sauces, potatoes, or rice. Here are three versions that go well with boiled cauliflower.

Cheese sauce

Make a roux with flour and butter, gradually add milk and vegetable bouillon, bring to a boil, then simmer. Stir in some grated Parmesan and sliced chives, and season with salt, pepper, and nutmeg.

Hollandaise

Make a roux with flour and butter and add a little bouillon. Gradually add milk, bringing to a boil each time. Season with salt, pepper, and nutmeg, simmer for 5 minutes, then combine 2 egg yolks with a little of the sauce and stir in.

Ham hollandaise

Add some finely diced boiled ham and sliced chives to the sauce to finish.

... with carrots, peas, and shrimp

Boil 1 cauliflower, broken into florets, for 15 minutes. Sweat 1 finely diced onion in butter, then add 11 oz (300 g) finely chopped carrot and 7 oz (200 g) frozen peas. Simmer with 2 cups (500 ml) vegetable bouillon for 5 minutes. Stir 2 tablespoons cornstarch into $^1/_2$ cup (125 ml) light cream then bring to a boil and season with salt and pepper. Mix thoroughly with the cauliflower and $4^1/_2$ oz (125 g) cooked shrimp, heat, and serve immediately.

... as tempura

Boil the florets of 1 cauliflower for about 10 minutes, until al dente. Combine 3 egg yolks with $^1/_2$ cup (125 ml) each water and white wine, generous 1 cup (150 g) all-purpose flour, salt, and nutmeg to make a batter; set aside for 10 minutes. Whisk 3 egg whites until stiff then fold into the batter. Dip the cauliflower florets in the batter then fry in hot oil for about 4 minutes. Drain on paper towels.

CAULIFLOWER
several variations

Cauliflower is also much used in Indian and Indonesian cuisine; here are two examples. The traditional partners are tomatoes, with their acidic flavor—and again you will find some tasty variations.

... with tomatoes, leek, and ginger

Finely chop 1 piece ginger and 1 chile, and sauté briefly in 2 tablespoons sesame oil. Add 7 oz (200 g) canned tomatoes and 1¼ cups (300 ml) vegetable bouillon, and season with turmeric, cumin, salt, and sugar. Add the florets of 1 cauliflower and, after 5 minutes, 2 sliced leeks. Cook for 10 minutes until al dente. Then stir in some cilantro leaves.

... breaded as schnitzels

Make several cuts in the stalk of 1 cauliflower, then cook the whole head in salt water until al dente. Cut into slices, a generous ½-in. (1-cm) thick. Separate 3 eggs. Whisk the egg whites until stiff. Combine the egg yolks with 1–2 teaspoons flour and season with salt. Fold into the beaten egg whites. Coat the cauliflower slices repeatedly and fry in hot oil until golden on both sides.

... au gratin with potatoes, ham, and cheese

Cook 1 cauliflower and generous 1 lb (500 g) sliced potatoes. Make a roux from 3 tablespoons flour and 4 tablespoons butter, then add ½ cup (125 ml) bouillon and generous 1½ cups (375 ml) milk. Simmer for 10 minutes. Stir in 7 tablespoons (50 g) grated Gouda, salt, pepper, and nutmeg. Layer the potatoes, cauliflower, and 13 oz (375 g) boiled ham in an ovenproof dish. Pour over the sauce and sprinkle with 7 tablespoons (50 g) grated Gouda. Bake at 400 °F/200 °C for 25 minutes.

... with peas, beefsteak tomatoes, and curry

Cook 1 cauliflower in florets for 10 minutes, until al dente. Place in an ovenproof dish with 2 chopped beefsteak tomatoes and 11 oz (300 g) blanched frozen peas, and season with salt and pepper. Sweat 1 diced onion with grated ginger and 2 chopped garlic cloves. Add 1 cup (250 ml) light cream and 2 teaspoons cornstarch, then season with salt, pepper, and 2 tablespoons each curry powder and lemon juice. Bake at 400 °F/200 °C.

KOHLRABI
with crème fraîche and parsley

Serves 4

1³/₄ lb (750g)	*kohlrabi*
	Salt
3 tbsp	*butter*
3 tbsp	*flour*
2 cups (500 ml)	*bouillon*
	Pepper
	Nutmeg
2 tbsp	*crème fraîche*
2 tbsp	*finely chopped parsley*

Step by step

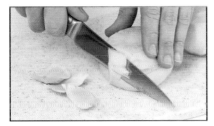

Peel and thinly slice the kohlrabi. Finely chop the leafy parts.

Slowly stir in the kohlrabi cooking water and bouillon, and simmer gently to reduce.

Cook the kohlrabi in salt water for 8–10 minutes until soft. Strain over a bowl, reserving the cooking water.

Season with salt, pepper, and nutmeg. Stir in the crème fraîche and add the kohlrabi.

Heat the butter in a small pan and make a roux with the flour. Cook until light brown.

Sprinkle with chopped parsley to serve.

KOHLRABI INFO

The first **kohlrabi**, also known as cabbage turnip, usually starts to appear in May. With over 30 white and 14 blue varieties, the

vegetable can be grown until well into November. There is no longer any need to fear the woody bulbs, since the popular varieties grow to a good size without becoming tough. If the leaves are still attached to the kohlrabi, their color and condition will tell you how fresh it is. Limp, yellow leaves indicate that the bulbs have already been in the store for several days. If the leaves have been removed, it may well be a little soft. Press against the root base—if you can feel any resistance, the bulb will be woody there.

CRÈME FRAÎCHE INFO

We differentiate between the various types of soured cream by their fat content. Soured cream has a minimum fat content of 10%, while **crème fraîche** contains at least 30% fat, and

may also contain up to 15% sucrose. Crème légère is a lighter version of crème fraîche, with an approximate fat content of 20%. Soured cream usually contains 20–29% fat, and binding agents may be used.

KOHLRABI

several variations

Kohlrabi is great for stuffing, but is also delicious as a vegetable with creamy sauces.

... with potatoes and cream cheese

Cut 6 potatoes into sticks and cook in boiling water. After about 3 minutes, add 1³/₄ lb (750 g) kohlrabi, also cut into sticks, and cook for 10–15 minutes. Strain, and reserve the cooking water. Stir 3 tablespoons butter, 5¹/₂ oz (150 g) cream cheese, 7 table-spoons (100 ml) light cream, and half the cooking water into the strained vegetables, then add a few of the chopped kohlrabi leaves. Season with nutmeg, salt, and pepper.

... deep fried in beer batter

Beat 2 eggs with generous ³/₄ cup (200 ml) Pilsner beer, stir in generous 1 cup (150 g) flour, and leave to stand for 15 minutes. Peel 1³/₄ lb (750 g) kohlrabi and cut into strips. Coat in beer batter and deep fry until golden.

... au gratin with cured pork

Dice 4 kohlrabi and cook in 2 cups (500 ml) bouillon for 10–15 minutes. Make a roux with 3 tablespoons each flour and butter, and add the cooking liquid. Combine 1 cup (250 ml) light cream with 2 egg yolks, then fold into the sauce with salt, pepper, sugar, and nutmeg. Place the kohlrabi pieces in an ovenproof dish and arrange 7 oz (200 g) finely chopped cured pork on top. Pour over the sauce and bake at 400 °F/200 °C for about 20 minutes.

... Hungarian style

Sauté 2¹/₂ oz (75 g) diced bacon and onion in 1 tablespoon ghee, then add 1 green bell pepper and 3 kohlrabi, all cut into strips. Season with 1 teaspoon sweet paprika, salt, and pepper. Stir in ¹/₂ cup (125 ml) vegetable bouillon and 2 tablespoons each tomato paste and tomato ketchup. Simmer for 20 minutes. Stir in 4 tablespoons soured cream and fold in 7 oz (200 g) sliced cabanossi (e.g. pepperoni). Sprinkle with parsley.

DIPS
for kohlrabi

Raw kohlrabi sticks are just as good for dipping as, for instance, celery stalks. Here are three dips to try:

Camembert and walnut dip
Mix chopped Camembert with white wine until creamy. Add some chopped walnuts and season with salt and pepper. Goes well with both raw and cooked kohlrabi.

Lemon and cress dip
Stir together generous $^3/_4$ cup (200 ml) soured cream, 1 cup (250 ml) yogurt, the grated rind of 1 organic lemon, salt, and pepper. Add 1 pack mustard cress to the dip.

Basil and cream cheese dip
Mix cream cheese with half-and-half cream. Stir in some grated garlic and finely chopped basil, and season with salt and pepper.

... as carpaccio
Blanch 14 oz (400 g) thinly sliced kohlrabi, arrange on a plate, and sprinkle with freshly grated pepper. Make a dressing of 3 tablespoons each olive oil and white wine vinegar, $1^1/_2$ teaspoons creamed horseradish, and water. Add pepper, salt, a pinch of sugar, and 3 tablespoons roughly chopped parsley to the sauce, and drizzle over the kohlrabi. Sprinkle with 3 tablespoons sunflower seeds.

... stuffed with tomato and goat's cheese
Hollow out 4 cooked kohlrabi and dice the flesh. Combine 1 bunch sliced scallions with $3^1/_2$ oz (100 g) crumbled goat's cheese, 7 tablespoons (100 ml) crème fraîche, the diced kohlrabi, and skinned and chopped tomatoes. Season with salt and pepper. Use to stuff the kohlrabi shells then place them, with any leftover mixture, in an ovenproof dish. Pour over 1 cup (250 ml) bouillon and bake at 400 °F/200 °C for about 15 minutes.

MUSHROOMS
r a g o u t   i n   c r e a m

Serves 4

generous 1 lb (500 g)	*portobello mushrooms*
7 tbsp	*butter*
2	*shallots, chopped*
	Salt
	Pepper
1 tsp	*cornstarch*
1 cup (250 ml)	*light cream*
¹/₂ bunch	*parsley, freshly chopped*

INFO

Mushrooms are often found growing wild in fields where horses graze, as they thrive in the manure. Mostly, however, they are grown in dark basements. There are very many varieties, although the most popular ones are those with white, pale pink, and brown heads. Mushrooms taste best when they are sautéed in a little butter with fresh herbs. They also go extremely well with all kinds of meat—sautéed, stewed, broiled, and grilled—and with most vegetables. And there's more good news—they have no cholesterol.

Step by step

Brush the mushrooms and wipe with a damp cloth.

Cut the mushrooms into quarters.

Heat 3 tablespoons butter in a skillet and sauté the shallots.

Add the mushrooms and the remainder of the butter, and sauté for 2 minutes. Season with salt and pepper.

Simmer until the liquid has evaporated. Stir the cornstarch into the cream, add to the mushrooms, and cook for a further 5 minutes.

Sprinkle with parsley to serve.

Side dish

Mashed potatoes with watercress make a tasty accompaniment for mushroom ragout. Cook 1³/₄ lb (800 g) potatoes in their skins, then drain and leave to cool a little. Peel, then push the potatoes through a ricer. Combine ¹/₂ cup (125 ml) warmed light cream with 1 tablespoon butter. Purée with 1¹/₂ bunch watercress (or parsley, dill, or chervil) in a blender. Stir into the potatoes and season with salt and pepper.

DIPS
for mushrooms

These dips with mustard, anchovies, and garlic go very well with all four variations.

Warm mayonnaise and mustard
Make a mayonnaise from egg yolk, peanut oil, lemon juice, salt, pepper, and Tabasco® Sauce, and stir in a bain marie until creamy. Add some mild mustard. Goes well with mushrooms au gratin.

Bacon and onion dip
Combine fried diced bacon and onion, cream, yogurt, lemon juice, chopped herbs, salt, pepper, and basil.

Aïoli
Stir together some crushed garlic, egg yolk, salt, pepper, and a little mustard. Add oil, drop by drop. Stir in some lemon juice. Dilute with a little soured cream and water if desired. Goes well with all recipe variations.

MUSHROOMS
several

There are so many different uses for cultivated mushrooms in the kitchen. Whether stuffed with vegetables, fish, meat, or grains; as a vegetarian patty, braised in port and au gratin, or simply coated in a beer batter and fried until crispy—the

... filled with tuna and chervil
Blanch 12 large mushrooms (stalks removed) for 3 minutes in $^1/_2$ cup (125 ml) each water and white wine, with salt, a bay leaf, pepper, and the grated rind of 1 lemon. Sprinkle with the lemon juice. Combine 2 tablespoons crème fraîche with 1 chopped shallot, 1 bunch chopped chervil, and 9 oz (250 g) drained tuna from a can. Season with salt and pepper. Spoon into the mushrooms.

... battered
Make a batter out of $^2/_3$ cup (100 g) all-purpose flour, $^1/_2$ cup (125 ml) milk, 1 egg yolk, salt, and pepper. Fold in one beaten egg white. Coat generous 1 lb (500 g) prepared mushrooms in the batter, and drain. Deep fry in hot oil at 350 °F/180 °C for a few minutes. Drain on paper towels. Serve hot.

variations

options are all equally delicious. Fried mushrooms make a perfect snack, side dish for a barbecue, or buffet accompaniment.

We have created six different dips that you can use and vary however you please.

... as patties

Finely chop generous 1 lb (500 g) prepared mushrooms. Mix with 1 chopped and sautéed onion, 2 tablespoons butter, 2 cups (100 g) dried breadcrumbs, 2 eggs, 2 tablespoons all-purpose flour, 4 slices white bread, diced, and 2 tablespoons soy sauce. Season with salt and pepper. Refrigerate for 30 minutes. Shape into patties with your hands, and fry in hot oil for 2–3 minutes each side until crisp.

... au gratin with port

Halve generous 1 lb (500 g) mushrooms—or leave whole if preferred—and sauté in 3 tablespoons butter. Season with salt and pepper, and leave to stand for 3 minutes. Fry 5 1/2 oz (150 g) chopped, smoked bacon, pour over 1/2 cup (125 ml) each port and light cream, and fold in the mushrooms. Simmer for 5 minutes. Spoon the mixture into 4 individual gratin dishes, sprinkle with 7 tablespoons (50 g) grated Gruyère, and dot with butter. Bake at 425 °F/220 °C for about 10 minutes.

DIPS
for mushrooms

Dips with herbs, hot mustard, or mango chutney also go well with mushrooms.

Cress dip

Combine soured cream, lemon juice, mustard cress or watercress, horseradish, salt, and pepper. Goes well with the stuffed, au gratin, and deep-fried mushroom recipes.

Hot mustard dip

Mix together some hot mustard, mustard powder, sugar, and vinegar. Add oil, drop by drop, and whisk until creamy. Stir in some chopped dill. Goes well with all recipe variations.

Mango and curry dip

Combine chopped apples, curry powder, and mango chutney. Goes well with deep-fried mushrooms and mushroom patties.

SUMMER

Summer is when most vegetables are harvested.

Thanks to the generous amount of sun they receive, they have an unbeatably intense aroma and plenty of healthy nutrients.

The following pages contain a small, but exclusive, selection of recipes and variations using summer vegetables.

There's bound to be something for you!

BROCCOLI
with vinaigrette

Serves 4

1³/₄ lb (750g)	*broccoli*
	Salt
2	*eggs, hard-boiled*
1	*gherkin*
2	*tomatoes*
6 tbsp	*oil*
2 tbsp	*mustard*
4 tbsp	*wine vinegar*
	Pepper
1	*onion, diced*
¹/₂ bunch	*chives, sliced*
¹/₂ bunch	*parsley, finely chopped*
1 tbsp	*dill, chopped*

Step by step

Wash and trim the broccoli, and break into rosettes. Peel and thinly slice the stalk.

Skin and deseed the tomatoes, then finely chop the flesh.

Cook the broccoli in boiling salt water for 10 minutes until al dente. Strain thoroughly.

Combine the remaining ingredients to make a vinaigrette.

Peel and chop the eggs, and finely dice the gherkin.

Carefully fold in the eggs, gherkin, and tomatoes. Arrange over the broccoli.

BROCCOLI INFO

Broccoli is a member of the brassica family, closely related to cauliflower, and the peeled stalk tastes a little like asparagus. It is also available with white, yellow, and pink rosettes—which are

every bit as delicious as the green ones. Broccoli is extremely healthy. It contains plenty of vitamin C, beta-carotene, and minerals such as zinc, potassium, and calcium. And the figure-conscious will be pleased to hear that 3¹/₂ oz (100 g) broccoli contain less than 30 kilocalories.

VINAIGRETTE INFO

Vinaigrette is a cold salad dressing made of a special vinegar ("vinaigre" in French), oil, and fresh herbs. The oil should also be of the very best quality, i.e. cold pressed. Top

chefs whisk the vinaigrette with a balloon whisk. As well as herbs, other ingredients such as shallots, capers, mustard, or finely chopped vegetables can be used to refine the dressing.

BROCCOLI
several variations

This aromatic vegetable really will enhance any cuisine. Whether steamed with a sauce, au gratin, in a curry or soup, or with pasta or rice—you'll be amazed by the variety of flavors. Opt for dark green, firm heads when shopping.

... as curry with coconut and cashew nuts

Heat 3 tablespoons red curry paste in a wok. Add 1 cup (250 ml) coconut milk, $1/4$ teaspoon soy sauce, 2 oz (60 g) baby corn, $4^1/_2$ oz (125 g) broccoli, $4^1/_2$ oz (125 g) blanched green beans, and 1 oz (25 g) cashews, and simmer for 10 minutes. Sprinkle over 1 tablespoon each chopped peanuts and basil, and serve.

... as risotto

Sweat a chopped shallot in butter. Add $1^1/_2$ cups (300 g) risotto rice, salt, pepper, 7 tablespoons (100 ml) white wine, and 3 cups (700 ml) vegetable bouillon, and simmer until the rice swells. Add generous 1 lb (500 g) broccoli and 12 oz (350 g) blanched green asparagus. Fold in 2 egg yolks, 3 tablespoons each light cream and chopped scallions, and $5^1/_2$ oz (150 g) diced boiled ham. Sprinkle with grated Gruyère and bake at 425 °F/220 °C for 15 minutes.

... as cream soup

Simmer $1^1/_2$ lb (700 g) broccoli for 15 minutes until soft, then blend to a purée. Stir in 3 tablespoons white wine and enough light cream to achieve a creamy consistency. Simmer gently for 5 minutes. Season to taste with salt, pepper, nutmeg, and a little cayenne. Serve garnished with 1 tablespoon crème fraîche and some slivers of roasted almond.

... on toast with egg and bell peppers

Cook generous 1 lb (500 g) broccoli rosettes in bouillon for 10 minutes. Drain. Place on toasted white bread. Make a creamy sauce from butter, flour, milk, salt, pepper, and nutmeg, and fold in chopped, hard-boiled egg. Pour over the broccoli and garnish with strips of bell pepper. Bake at 425 °F/220 °C for 25 minutes.

SAUCES
for broccoli

You can vary these sauces for gratins or boiled broccoli, to suit your taste.

Ham and cheese sauce

Make a roux from butter and flour, then add vegetable bouillon to make a sauce. Season to taste with salt, pepper, and nutmeg. Stir in grated cheese and simmer gently. Fold in the diced ham. Goes well with steamed broccoli.

Ginger and cilantro butter sauce

Sauté grated root ginger in plenty of hot butter and oil. Deglaze the pan with lemon juice and grated lemon rind, then fold in the chopped cilantro. Goes well with gratins, and steamed broccoli.

Parsley and crab sauce

Sauté chopped shallot in butter. Dust with flour, then add enough broth to make a creamy sauce. Stir in lemon juice and chopped parsley. Season to taste with salt, pepper, and chile powder. Fold in the crab meat. Goes well with cooked broccoli, toast, and gratin.

... Italian-style with anchovies

Sweat 1 chopped onion, 1 chopped garlic clove, and 5 chopped anchovies in 3 tablespoons oil. Add 1¹/₂ lb (700 g) steamed broccoli. Place in a greased gratin dish and top with 5¹/₂ oz (150 g) sliced mortadella and 3 tablespoons chopped parsley. Combine 1 cup (250 ml) light cream with eggs, pepper, nutmeg, and 2 tablespoons grated Parmesan, and pour over. Bake at 425 °F/220 °C for 40 minutes.

... as pistachio and Ricotta pasta sauce

Cook generous 1 lb (500 g) broccoli rosettes for 10 minutes until al dente, then drain. Sauté 1 chopped shallot in oil, and add a quarter of the chopped broccoli rosettes. Stir in 1²/₃ cups (400 ml) bouillon, 3¹/₂ oz (100 g) Ricotta, and 1 oz (25 g) ground pistachios. Season to taste with salt, pepper, and lemon juice. Fold in 1 tablespoon capers and the remainder of the broccoli. Sprinkle with pistachios.

CELERY
with filbert butter

INFO

Celery, is a composite flower plant, also known as branch celery. It is covered with soil or paper to bleach it and make it even more aromatic. Self-bleaching celery is now available. The stalks are 12–16 in. (30–40 cm) long; they are used as a side dish, raw in salads or for dips, and in soups. The ground seeds are used in celery salt. The celery season begins in July and ends in November.

Serves 4

3	*celery stalks*
	Salt
5 tbsp	*butter*
5 tbsp	*grated filberts*
	Pepper

Step by step

Trim and wash the celery, and halve or quarter the stalks.

Bring some water and 1 teaspoon of salt to a boil in a pan.

Place the celery in the boiling water and cook for about 10 minutes, until al dente.

Melt the butter in a skillet and allow it to brown.

Fry the filberts in the butter until golden. Drain the celery. Season with salt and pepper, and pour over the nut butter.

Side dish

Potato purée with cumin: boil 1³/₄ lb (800 g) unpeeled potatoes in salt water until soft. Drain, and leave until no longer steaming. Peel and push through a ricer. Blend with 7 tablespoons (100 ml) milk. Stir 2 tablespoons butter and 1 tablespoon cumin into the purée. Season to taste with salt, pepper, and nutmeg. Goes well with breaded schnitzels.

Side dish

To make a **mushroom risotto**, sweat 1¹/₄ cups (250 g) risotto rice and 1 chopped onion in 2 tablespoons olive oil. Add 1 cup (250 ml) white wine, and simmer until absorbed. Gradually add 2 cups (500 ml) bouillon, stirring frequently until the rice is soft and creamy. Season with salt and pepper. Trim and wipe 9 oz (250 g) common-store or other mushrooms (or use soaked bolete), then dice and sauté in 1 tablespoon butter. Stir into the risotto just before the end of the cooking time.

SAUCES
for celery

Three sauces to add a creamy, spicy or savory touch to celery stalks:

Sauce hollandaise Mousseline

Make a sauce from chopped shallot, white wine vinegar, white wine, egg yolk, butter, lemon juice, salt, and cayenne, and fold in whisked light whipping cream. Goes with braised celery stalks.

Sherry sauce

Stir cornstarch into water and combine with soy sauce, sherry, honey, and Tabasco® Sauce. Goes with pasta, and celery stalks.

Meat sauce

Sauté chopped onion and garlic in herb butter. Stir in ground beef or other meat, tomato paste, meat bouillon, chopped celery leaves, and crème fraîche. Goes with celery stalks, and pecan nuts.

... braised with wine and garlic, for meat

Cut 6 celery stalks 6 in. (15 cm) above the root, and boil in salt water for 10 minutes. Sauté 1 chopped onion and garlic in oil. Add the cooked celery, and season with salt and pepper. Add 1 cup (250 ml) wine and $^1/_2$ cup (125 ml) vegetable bouillon. Bake at 350 °F/180 °C for 45 minutes. Quarter the celery hearts, and serve with the reduced cooking juices.

... with tomatoes, ham, and cheese, for fish

Cut generous 1 lb (500 g) celery stalks into 2-in. (5-cm) chunks and cook in $1^1/_4$ cups (300 ml) bouillon for 10 minutes. Drain and place in a gratin dish. Cut 5 tomatoes into slices. Arrange on the celery. Arrange 4 slices boiled ham on top, and sprinkle over 7 tablespoons (50 g) grated Emmental. Bake at 425 °F/220 °C for 10 minutes.

CELERY
several variations

Crisp celery stalks can be used in lots of different ways. Try them braised or au gratin, stuffed, or raw with tasty dips. When shopping, make sure the stalks are firm and light green in color.

... baked with pecan nuts, for lamb

Slice 1 bunch celery, and place in a gratin dish with $1/2$ teaspoon each cumin and coriander, 1 chopped garlic clove, 1 chopped onion, and $1^3/4$ oz (50 g) halved pecan nuts. Combine $2/3$ cup (150 ml) each bouillon and light cream, and season with salt and pepper. Sprinkle over 1 cup (50 g) dried breadcrumbs and 1 oz (30 g) grated Parmesan. Bake at 400 °F/200 °C for 40 minutes.

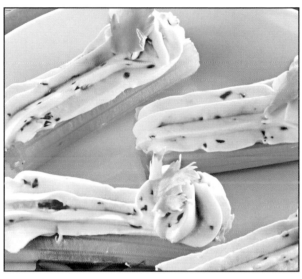

... stuffed with cream cheese

Halve generous 1 lb (500 g) large celery stalks and cut into 4-in. (10-cm) long pieces. Combine $5^1/2$ oz (150 g) ewe's milk cheese with $3^1/2$ oz (100 g) each cream cheese and yogurt, 3 tablespoons milk, 2 tablespoons brandy, and 1 teaspoon mustard. Season with salt and pepper. Stir in $1/4$ finely chopped red bell pepper. Spoon the cream into a pastry bag, and pipe it along the hollow lengths of the celery stalks.

... with carrots, bell peppers, and sugar snap peas, for pasta

Chop 1 onion, 3 celery stalks, and 1 red and 1 green bell pepper into small pieces, and sauté in 2 tablespoons olive oil. Dice 2 carrots and blanch with $4^1/2$ oz (125 g) baby corn and $1^3/4$ oz (50 g) sugar snap peas. Stir into the sautéed vegetables. Fold into cooked pasta.

... in batter

Cut generous 1 lb (500 g) celery stalks into 2-in. (5-cm) pieces and cook in $1^1/4$ cups (300 ml) vegetable bouillon for 5–10 minutes until al dente. Drain thoroughly. Make a batter from $1^1/3$ cups (200 g) all-purpose flour, 2 egg yolks, and 1 cup (250 ml) milk, then fold in two whisked egg whites. Season with salt, pepper, and nutmeg. Dip the celery in the batter and fry in hot oil.

FAVA BEANS INFO

Fava beans, also known as broad beans, are the dried seeds of the bean pod. They are soaked in water overnight and then cooked on the following day. Once a year, however, in the summer, these delightful beans are available fresh. The actual seeds

lie in a soft, white "bed" inside a thick, fleshy pod. The skin on the outside of the beans has a very high tannin content, and therefore tastes bitter. Botanically, they are a vetch. When buying these beans, allow for twice the quantity you actually need, since about half the weight consists of the pods. The pods are split open and the beans removed. It is easier to remove the skin around them after they have been cooked. The beans can safely be eaten raw once the outer skins have been removed. They have a very strong flavor. To peel uncooked fava beans, pour boiling water over them, then dip them in cold water, and remove the skins.

Fava beans can be braised in butter, puréed, and served in salads. They harmonize with parsley, savory, dill, and chervil, and go well with beef, veal, pork, lamb, and mutton. They also make an excellent vegetable, particularly when served in a cream sauce.

Serves 4

14 oz (400 g)	*fava beans, hulled, about. 3¹/₄ lb (1.5 kg) unpeeled weight*
3¹/₂ oz (100 g)	*streaky bacon*
2 tbsp	*butter*
3	*shallots, diced*
	Salt
	Pepper
¹/₂ bunch	*flat-leafed parsley, chopped*
¹/₂ bunch	*savory, chopped*

Step by step

Blanch the beans in boiling water for 3–4 minutes, then pour off the water and drain.

Fry the chopped bacon until crispy, then drain off the fat.

Carefully remove the tough skins from half the beans.

Melt the butter and sauté the shallots.

Finely chop the bacon.

Sweat the unpeeled beans for 6 minutes first, then the peeled ones. Season, then stir into the herbs and bacon.

FAVA BEANS
with bacon

SIDE DISHES
for fava beans

Potato purée goes well with fava beans, and can be prepared in lots of different ways.

Potato purée with ham

Make a purée of 1³/₄ lb (800 g) potatoes in their skins, flavor with tarragon, and stir in some very finely chopped, briefly sautéed, diced ham.

Potato purée with curry

Cook 1³/₄ lb (800 g) potatoes in their skins, then peel and push through a ricer. Stir in some fried onions, curry powder, milk, sesame oil, salt, pepper, and a little sugar. Scatter over some sesame seeds, if desired.

Potato purée with nuts

Cook 1³/₄ lb (800 g) potatoes in their skins, then peel and push through a ricer. Mix with some milk, butter, hazelnut oil, and chopped filberts. Scatter over some chopped scallions, if desired.

FAVA BEANS
several

For a long time, fava beans—also called broad, field, bell, or tic beans—were used as animal fodder rather than for human consumption. That, however, was doing these delightful beans a great disservice. It is important to remove the tough skin around the

... with tagliatelle

Sauté 1 chopped onion and 1 chopped garlic clove in oil. Stir in 1 cup (250 ml) vegetable bouillon, ¹/₂ teaspoon saffron, and 1 cup (250 ml) light cream. Reduce by a half. Add 9 oz (250 g) blanched fava beans, 1 diced red bell pepper, and 1 sliced red chile, and season with salt and pepper. Combine with 11 oz (300 g) cooked tagliatelle and chopped thyme.

... as risotto

Sauté 1³/₄ lb (50 g) diced bacon in 1 tablespoon oil. Add 7 oz (200 g) chanterelles and continue frying. Stir in 2 sliced scallions, 12 oz (350 g) fava beans, previously blanched and skinned, and season with salt and pepper. Sweat 1¹/₂ cups (300 g) risotto rice with chopped onion and garlic in 1 tablespoon oil. Add 3³/₄ cups (900 ml) chicken bouillon and simmer until the rice has cooked. Fold in the bean mixture and chopped parsley. Season to taste.

v a r i a t i o n s

beans, as this reveals the delicate seeds that now also have their place in exclusive cuisine, as you will see from the variations offered here.

... in lamb ragout

Brown 1 lb (500 g) sliced lamb shoulder in olive oil. Add 2 chopped onions, 1 pack diced casserole vegetables, and 1 sprig rosemary and cook briefly. Deglaze the pan with $^1/_2$ cup (125 ml) each red wine and vegetable bouillon. Bake in the oven for about 1 hour. Cut the meat into bite-sized pieces. Strain the cooking juices, and bind with flour and butter. Bring to a boil with 11 oz (300 g) blanched fava beans, $3^1/_2$ oz (100 g) shallots, salt, pepper, and parsley.

... Asian style with duck breasts

Marinate strips of duck breast in 3 tablespoons each soy sauce and chicken bouillon and $1^1/_2$ tablespoons cornstarch, then brown in hot oil. Add 11 oz (300 g) skinned fava beans, 2 chopped red chiles, 7 oz (200 g) carrot batons, and 1 teaspoon freshly ground ginger. Deglaze with generous $^3/_4$ cup (200 ml) orange juice, and reduce. Season to taste with salt and pepper. Stir in $1^3/_4$ oz (50 g) peanuts.

SIDE DISHES
for fava beans

Try these side dishes with fava beans.

Potato omelet

Make a filling from sliced potato, carrots, and tomatoes for an omelet of beaten eggs, salt, pepper, ground paprika, chopped scallions, and chile powder.

Falafel

Shape a mixture of puréed chickpeas, cooked bulgur wheat, sautéed, diced onion and garlic, chopped parsley, bouillon, salt, cumin, and chile powder into balls, and deep fry until golden.

Rice and turmeric

Sweat 2 cups (400 g) rice in oil, then simmer in double the quantity of water, a little salt, and turmeric.

ZUCCHINI
pan-fried with tomatoes and herbs

INFO

Zucchini—the word comes from the Italian for "little marrows"—really is a marrow, even though it looks more like a cucumber. Its flesh, however, is firmer and more aromatic than a cucumber's, and tastes best if the vegetable is harvested while still unripe, i.e. when no more than about 8 in. (20 cm) in length. The riper they are, the less flavor they have. Zucchini (the singular is zucchino, but it is usual to refer to them in the plural) are available in green and yellow. They are delicious served in lots of ways—raw, braised, boiled, etc. The flowers are also edible, and can be stuffed and fried.

Serves 4

14 oz (400 g)	zucchini
11 oz (300 g)	tomatoes
1	garlic clove, chopped
1/2 bunch	scallions, sliced
2 tbsp	olive oil
	Salt
	Pepper
1 tbsp	oregano, freshly chopped
1 tbsp	basil, freshly chopped

Step by step

Wash the zucchini, trim the ends, and cut into slices.

Wash the tomatoes, remove the stalks, and cut into eighths.

Sauté the garlic and scallions in hot oil.

Add the tomatoes and zucchini, and simmer for 5–10 minutes. Season with salt and pepper.

Sprinkle with the herbs and serve immediately.

Side dish

To make **baked polenta**, bring 3¼ cups (750 ml) salt water to a boil, and slowly pour in 9 oz (250 g) semolina. Stir until smooth. Leave the polenta to simmer for about 20 minutes, stirring frequently, until a spoon stays upright in it. Smooth the polenta out onto a floured surface and leave to cool. Cut polenta pieces out of the mix and fry in hot butter until golden.

Side dish

Pour 2 cups (500 ml) vegetable bouillon over 1¼ cups (250 g) **couscous** and leave to expand for 20 minutes. Finely chop 1 red bell pepper and sauté in 1 tablespoon oil. Toast 3½ oz (100 g) cashews dry in a skillet. Stir the bell pepper and cashews into the couscous. Season with salt, pepper, and chopped cilantro.

SUMMER

SAUCES
for zucchini

You simply must try these sauces! Exotic, or with fresh herbs, they make the perfect accompaniments for zucchini.

Cilantro and cashew sauce

Sauté chopped onion and garlic in oil. Purée with roasted cashew, chopped cilantro, cumin, grated coconut, sugar, and yogurt. Goes well with grilled or broiled skewers, and tofu pan fry.

Herb sauce

Sweat chopped shallot in butter. Pour over white wine and vegetable bouillon, and reduce slightly. Add sour cream and simmer. Stir in some chopped mixed herbs and lemon juice. Season with salt and pepper. Goes well with zucchini skewers, and soufflé.

Tomato sauce

Make a sauce out of diced bacon, chopped onion, casserole vegetables, tomato, bouillon, red wine, chopped oregano and basil, salt, and pepper. Purée. Goes well with zucchini in bacon, and skewers.

... in bacon

Blanch 4 whole zucchini in boiling salt water for 5 minutes. Drain and halve lengthwise. Mix together 3 tablespoons tomato paste, 1 teaspoon grated lemon rind, and 3 tablespoons chopped thyme, and smooth over the zucchini halves. Season with salt and pepper, and push the halves back together. Wrap bacon rashers around each zucchini, and bake in the oven at 400 °F/200 °C for 15 minutes.

... as flatbread

Grate 11 oz (300 g) zucchini onto paper towels. Drain, then combine with $1/2$ chopped red chile, $2/3$ cup (100 g) all-purpose flour, 2 eggs, 3 tablespoons milk, 2 tablespoons chopped thyme, salt, and pepper. Fry flatbreads until crisp in 3 tablespoons oil. Serve hot.

ZUCCHINI
several variations

Whether served raw or cooked, this fabulous vegetable tastes of summer, sun, and healthy freshness. Try it in all the different variants—in soufflé, flatbread, chicken and vegetable skewers, or wrapped in bacon—and become a zucchini fan. Incidentally, the plants are very easy to grow in the garden, or even on a balcony.

... as tortilla with egg and goat's cheese

Sauté 1 chopped garlic clove in butter, then add 5½ oz (150 g) finely grated, squeezed zucchini, 1 tablespoon roasted pine nuts, and a little grated lemon rind, and simmer. Season with salt and pepper. Whisk 3 eggs and fry in 2 tablespoons hot oil, until just set. Combine the zucchini mix with 2 oz (60 g) goat's cheese and place on top of the eggs. Bake in the oven at 350 °F/180 °C for 10 minutes.

... as soufflé

Purée 11 oz (300 g) cooked zucchini and combine with 2 egg yolks. Fry 1¾ oz (50 g) oatmeal in 2 tablespoons butter. Stir in 7 tablespoons (100 ml) milk and generous ¾ cup (200 ml) vegetable bouillon. Season with salt and pepper, and stir in 2 tablespoons chopped chervil. Fold in 2 beaten egg whites. Spoon into little moulds, and bake in the oven at 400 °F/200 °C for 20–25 minutes.

... as chicken and vegetable skewers

Place 11 oz (300 g) chicken breast pieces, 1 red and 1 yellow bell pepper cut into pieces, 6 oz (175 g) mushrooms, and 1 sliced zucchini on soaked wooden skewers. Combine 3 tablespoons lemon juice, 1 teaspoon grated lemon rind, 3 tablespoons olive oil, salt, and pepper, and brush over the skewers. Barbecue or broil for 20 minutes, then brush with the marinade and sprinkle with parsley.

... with tofu

Heat 3 tablespoons peanut oil in a wok, and fry 5½ oz (150 g) diced tofu until crispy. Remove and drain thoroughly. Sauté 1 tablespoon freshly grated ginger in the remainder of the oil. Sauté generous 1 lb (500 g) diced zucchini, and 1 red and 1 yellow bell pepper, diced, for 3 minutes. Season with salt and pepper, and stir in 2 tablespoons oyster sauce. Add the tofu and drizzle with sesame oil.

BELL PEPPER INFO

How to skin **bell peppers**, step by step:

Halve the peppers, then wash and place them, skin side up, on a baking sheet. Brush with oil.

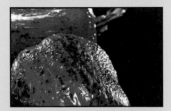

Place under a hot broiler until the skin darkens and starts to blister.

Remove the bell peppers from the broiler and place in a plastic bag. Seal the bag and leave to cool.

Remove the bell peppers from the bag and lift off the skins.

Serves 4

1 each	red, yellow, and green bell pepper
2 tbsp	olive oil
1	onion, chopped
1	garlic clove, chopped
7 tbsp (100 ml)	white wine
	Salt
	Pepper
2 tbsp	herbes de Provence

Step by step

Trim and deseed the bell peppers, then wash and cut into strips.

Heat the olive oil and sauté the onion and garlic.

Add the bell peppers and sweat for 5 minutes.

Pour over the wine and simmer until it has almost completely evaporated.

Season the bell peppers with salt and pepper.

Sprinkle the herbes de Provence over the vegetables.

BELL PEPPERS
Mediterranean style with herbes de Provence

BELL PEPPERS
several variations

Bell peppers are available in several different colors, and can be used in many different ways. Try them all, and see which is your favorite!

... with ground meat

Remove the tops from and deseed 8 bell peppers. Make a filling from 11 oz (300 g) ground meat, 1 chopped onion, and $^1/_2$ bunch chopped fresh parsley, and season with salt, pepper, and dried parsley. Stir in 3$^1/_2$ oz (100 g) cooked rice. Spoon into the bell peppers and place them in an ovenproof dish. Replace the tops on the bell peppers. Pour over 2 cups (500 ml) bouillon. Cover and bake for 30 minutes at 350 °F/180 °C.

... as peperonata

Sweat $^3/_4$ oz (20 g) softened raisins, 2 chopped onions and garlic cloves, and 1 chopped red chile in 3 tablespoons olive oil. Add 2 tablespoons honey, $^2/_3$ cup (150 ml) vegetable bouillon, and 2 tablespoons sherry vinegar, and reduce by a half. Skin and dice 2 red and 2 yellow bell peppers, then add to the pan and heat. Serve hot or cold.

... as a vegetable with tofu and coconut

Chop 2$^1/_4$ lb (1 kg) mixed bell peppers and sweat in oil with chopped onions, garlic, and bamboo shoots for 7 minutes. Deglaze the pan with 7 tablespoons (100 ml) bouillon, and reduce a little. Add 2 chopped mild chiles. Stir in 1 cup (250 ml) coconut milk, and simmer until creamy. Fold in 3$^1/_2$ oz (100 g) bean sprouts and 7 oz (200 g) fried tofu cubes. Season with salt and coriander.

... with polenta filling

Blanch 12 bell peppers in salt water for 6 minutes, then leave to cool. Combine $^2/_3$ cup (100 g) cornmeal and 1$^2/_3$ cups (400 ml) vegetable bouillon to make polenta. Stir in 2 tablespoons butter and 3 tablespoons soft cream cheese with herbs (e.g. Boursin®). Spoon into a pastry bag. Working from top to bottom, carefully scoop the seeds and ribs from the bell peppers. Pipe in the filling. Drizzle with oil. Broil for 10 minutes and season with salt and pepper.

SIDE DISHES
for bell peppers

Fresh bread is the best accompaniment for all dishes—not least because it can be used to mop up the very last traces of the delicious sauce!

Baguette

Combine $1^1/_2$ tablespoons (15 g) yeast, $2^1/_2$ cups (375 g) wheat flour, 1 cup (250 ml) warm water, and $1^1/_2$ teaspoons salt into a dough and leave to rise. Shape into loaves and brush with beaten egg. Make diagonal cuts in the surface. Place on a baking sheet in the oven, with a pan of water on the shelf below. Bake at 425 °F/220 °C for 35 minutes.

Ciabatta

Combine $1^1/_4$ teaspoons (5 g) yeast, 3 tablespoons milk, a little sugar, $3^1/_2$ cups (500 g) strong white flour, and $^1/_2$ teaspoon salt into a dough and leave to rise for 30 minutes. Knead in 1 tablespoon olive oil, and leave for 2 more hours until bubbles start to form on the surface. Halve the dough and shape into loaves. Place on a greased baking sheet and bake at 425 °F/220 °C for 30 minutes.

Granary bread

Combine 1 yeast block, $1^1/_4$ cups (300 ml) warm water, 2 cups (300 g) strong white flour, $1^1/_3$ cups (200 g) spelt flour, generous $^1/_2$ cup (100 g) mixed grains, 2 teaspoons salt, and 2 tablespoons olive oil into a dough. Leave to rise, then shape into long loaves, and brush the surface with water. Bake at 400 °F/200 °C for 40 minutes.

... as lesco

Sauté $1^3/_4$ oz (50 g) diced smoked bacon, 1 chopped onion, and 1 chopped garlic clove in a little butter. Sprinkle over 1 tablespoon ground paprika. Add $1^3/_4$ oz (50 g) each diced red and green bell pepper, and simmer for 3 minutes. Add $1^3/_4$ lb (750 g) skinned, diced tomatoes, and simmer for a further 3 minutes. Season with salt and pepper.

... marinated in olive oil

Skin 3 red and 1 green bell peppers (see page 70), and cut into strips about 1 in. (3 cm) wide. Place half in a shallow dish. Season with salt and pepper, then combine 1 bunch chopped parsley with 4 finely chopped garlic cloves. Spread half over the bell peppers. Cover with the remainder of the bell peppers. Spread the other half of the parsley mixture on top. Pour over $^1/_2$ cup (125 ml) olive oil. Cover, and leave for 12 hours.

GREEN BEANS
with nut breadcrumbs

INFO

Green beans is the collective term for garden beans. They are available as runner beans, string beans, wax beans, and haricot vert. The latter is a young, very slender green bean with a delicate flavor and no strings. None should be eaten raw as they are toxic. Although phasin is destroyed by cooking, certain sugars that cause gas are not. This is where cumin, savory, and mustard can come to the rescue. What makes beans particularly valuable is their very high protein content.

Serves 4

14 oz (400 g)	green beans
	Salt
5 tbsp	butter
1 cup (50 g)	breadcrumbs
²/₃ cup (50 g)	filberts, chopped

Step by step

Trim and wash the beans, and pull off any stringy bits.

Boil in salt water for 15 minutes. Pour off the water, and leave the beans to drain.

Melt the butter in a pan.

Fry the breadcrumbs and chopped nuts until golden.

Sprinkle over the beans, and serve.

Side dish

Patties go extremely well with green beans. Combine generous 1 lb (500 g) ground beef with 1–2 slightly stale rolls, soaked and squeezed out. Add 1–2 eggs, salt, pepper, ground paprika, herbes de Provence, and 1 chopped onion, and combine well. Shape into 8–10 patties, and fry well on both sides in hot oil.

Side dish

Beans wrapped in bacon is a well-known dish—and prepared in the same way—but have you ever tried **potatoes wrapped in bacon**? Cook about 1³/₄ lb (800 g) small, waxy potatoes in their skins until al dente. Drain, cool slightly, then peel. Place 1 oregano stem on each potato, and wrap around $1/_2$ slice bacon. Secure with a cocktail pick. Heat 3 tablespoons oil in a pan and fry the potatoes on all sides until crispy.

GREEN BEANS
several variations

Steamed, crisp green beans go very well with fish, poultry, and meat, and are also excellent in soups and stews, gratins, or prepared Mediterranean–style.

... au gratin, with ham

Fry 1^3/$_4$ lb (50 g) diced bacon until the fat has run. Add 1 chopped onion and garlic clove, 4 oz (120 g) boiled ham cut into strips, and 1^1/$_4$ lb (600 g) chopped, cooked green beans, and simmer for 3 minutes. Place in a greased ovenproof dish. Whisk together 3 eggs with generous ^{3}/$_4$ cup (200 ml) sour cream, 4 tablespoons grated Gruyère, salt, pepper, and ground paprika, and pour over the top. Bake at 400 °F/200 °C for 25 minutes.

... with tomato pesto and Parmesan

Blanch 14 oz (400 g) green beans in salt water for 10 minutes, then drain and halve. Sweat with 1 chopped onion in 2 tablespoons oil. Season with salt and pepper. Combine with a pesto made from tomatoes, garlic, pine nuts, Parmesan, and oil, and serve with grated Parmesan, roasted pine nuts, and hand-shredded basil.

... with sun-dried tomatoes

Sauté 2 oz (50 g) diced bacon in 1 tablespoon oil until crisp. Add 1 chopped garlic clove and 1 tablespoon chopped rosemary. Stir in generous 1 lb (500 g) cooked and halved green beans and 3 oz (80 g) drained sun-dried tomatoes cut into strips, and simmer for 5 minutes. Season with salt and pepper.

... in mutton stew

Braise 1 chopped onion and garlic clove with 1^3/$_4$ lb (800 g) diced mutton. Season with salt and pepper. Simmer gently in 4 cups (1 liter) bouillon with 2 bay leaves for 30 minutes. Add generous 1 lb (500 g) halved green beans, 14 oz (400 g) each peeled and diced potatoes and carrots, 4^1/$_2$ oz (125 g) peeled and diced celeriac, then stir in 7 oz (200 g) skinned and chopped tomatoes, chopped savory, and marjoram.

SAUCES
for green beans

Whether the beans are being served as a vegetable or side dish, one of these sauces will go perfectly with them.

Curried yogurt sauce
Sweat chopped ginger, chile, and onion, then add curry powder and vegetable bouillon and simmer. Combine yogurt with flour, and use to bind the sauce. Goes well with steamed beans.

Mustard and caper sauce
Sauté a chopped onion, then dust with flour, and add chicken bouillon and light cream to make a sauce. Bring to a boil and stir in some mustard. Fold in the drained capers and season with salt and pepper. Goes well with beans au gratin and with fish.

Egg sauce
Make a roux from butter and flour. Add 2 cups (500 ml) vegetable bouillon, simmer to make a smooth sauce, and reduce by a third. Stir in some white wine and season with salt, pepper, and lemon. Fold in hard-boiled eggs and sliced chives. Goes well with beans and ham.

... au gratin, with tuna
Sauté 1 chopped onion and garlic clove in 1 tablespoon oil. Add 1 red bell pepper cut into strips, 9 oz (250 g) drained, canned sweet corn, and 14 oz (400 g) chopped green beans, and season with salt and pepper. Add 1 tablespoon chopped thyme. Place in a greased oven-proof dish and spread 11 oz (300 g) drained, canned tuna on top. Top with béchamel sauce, and bake at 400 °F/200 °C for 30 minutes.

... with fish fillets
Poach 4 fish fillets, each weighing $5^1/_2$ oz (150 g), and sprinkle over 1 tablespoon vinegar. Top with onion rings and pour over $^1/_2$ cup (125 ml) light cream. Trim $1^3/_4$ lb (750 g) green beans and cook in boiling salt water for 15 minutes, until al dente. Pour off the water, and leave the beans to drain. Pour over 4 tablespoons melted butter and 2 tablespoons freshly chopped parsley. Serve with the fish fillets.

TOMATOES
with olives

Serves 4

1	onion, chopped
¹/₂ tsp	sugar
¹/₂ cup (120 ml)	olive oil
3 tbsp	dry white wine
11 oz (300 g)	tomatoes, skinned and chopped
	Salt
	Pepper
1 tbsp	thyme, freshly chopped
3¹/₂ oz (100 g)	black olives, pitted

Step by step

Sauté the onions and sugar in hot olive oil.

Season with salt and pepper, and stir in the thyme.

Pour over the wine and simmer until almost evaporated.

Finely chop the black olives with a knife.

Add the tomatoes and simmer for 5 minutes.

Stir the chopped olives into the tomatoes.

TOMATOES INFO

Lots of recipes call for **skinned tomatoes**. Peeling them with a knife would take far too much time, and would also be quite wasteful. The better option is to place them in boiling water, and the skins almost come away by themselves. All you have to do

is to cut out the core with a sharp knife, and cut a slit in the skin on the opposite side. Then

dip the tomatoes, either singly or in batches, in boiling water. As soon as the skin around the slit starts to roll back, remove the tomatoes and run them under

cold water. Pull off the skin with a small knife.

SAUCES
made from tomatoes

Pasta is a classic companion for tomatoes. Try these three tomato-based sauces.

Tomato and ground beef sauce

Fry ground beef and diced bacon with diced casserole vegetables until the meat starts to crumble. Pour over some wine and add tomatoes and their juice, then season and simmer for 20 minutes. Sprinkle with fresh thyme.

Tomato and apple sauce

Sweat a chopped onion in malt vinegar. Add chopped apple and tomatoes, and stir in some raisins. Season to taste with salt, pepper, chile powder, cardamom, ginger, coriander, and sugar.

Spicy tomato sauce

Simmer together a chopped onion, garlic, canned tomatoes with basil, oregano, nutmeg, Tabasco® Sauce, soy sauce, hot ground paprika, salt, and pepper for 30 minutes. Purée.

... with prawns and white beans

Sauté 16 halved prawns in 3 tablespoons oil, then remove from the pan. Sauté 2 chopped onions and 2 chopped garlic cloves in the oil. Add 1 tablespoon tomato paste, $^2/_3$ cup (150 ml) orange juice, $1^1/_2$ lb (700 g) drained, canned white beans, and 1 chopped red chile. Simmer for 5 minutes. Stir in generous 1 lb (500 g) skinned tomato quarters, 1 bunch shredded basil, and the prawns. Cook for 3 minutes. Season to taste.

... au gratin, with anchovies

Arrange 8 skinned tomato halves in a gratin dish. Season with salt and pepper. Combine 8 drained anchovy fillets, 2 chopped shallots, 2 chopped hard-boiled eggs, $^1/_2$ bunch each chopped chervil and parsley, 2 tablespoons herbes de Provence, and 3 tablespoons dried breadcrumbs, and spoon over the tomatoes. Drizzle over 4 tablespoons olive oil, and bake at 400 °F/200 °C for 15 minutes.

TOMATOES
several variations

Tomatoes are so versatile that preparing them in lots of different ways is easy. The recipes shown here are just a few suggestions. Let your imagination run wild!

... as salsa, with grilled meat and fish

Skin and deseed generous 1 lb (500 g) tomatoes, then chop into tiny pieces, saving the juice. Season with salt and 2 teaspoons Tabasco® Sauce. Dice 1 red bell pepper and finely chop 2 onions and 2 garlic cloves. Finely chop 2 green chiles with their seeds, and 2 deseeded red ones. Combine well. Season to taste with salt, pepper, 1 pinch sugar, 1 tablespoon lemon juice, and 1 tablespoon apple vinegar. Purée a quarter of the mixture, then combine with the chopped vegetables.

... as a cream soup

Sweat 2 packs chopped casserole vegetables, 1 chopped onion, and 1 teaspoon dried marjoram in 2 tablespoons olive oil. Pour over 2 cups (500 ml) vegetable bouillon. Add $1^3/_4$ lb (800 g) canned tomatoes and season with salt and pepper. Simmer for 30 minutes, then purée, strain through a sieve, and season with sugar. Stir in $1^3/_4$ oz (50 g) diced bacon and sliced chives. Serve garnished with a spoon of whisked, heavy whipping cream.

... grilled or broiled with ewe's milk cheese

Oil 4 pieces of aluminum foil, then sprinkle with salt and pepper. Slice 2 onions and generous 1 lb (500 g) beefsteak tomatoes (reserving 8 slices), then season with salt and pepper. Place 4 slices ewe's milk cheese, each weighing about $5^1/_2$ oz (150 g) on top, and then the sliced tomatoes. Arrange 6 pitted black olives on each portion, and top with shredded basil. Fold the foil up into parcels. Place on a barbecue or under the broiler and cook for 15–20 minutes.

... with veal

Cut "hats" off 4 beefsteak tomatoes. Scoop out the seeds, then season the tomato shells with salt and leave to drain. Fry 3 slices white bread (without crusts) and 7 oz (200 g) ground veal in 4 tablespoons butter. Add 2 chopped garlic cloves, then stir in $1^1/_3$ cups (150 g) grated Gruyère. Spoon the filling into the tomatoes. Place on a greased baking sheet. Bake at 430 °F/225 °C for 20 minutes.

FENNEL
INFO

Fennel has two uses in the kitchen. The bulb is used as a vegetable and consumed raw, steamed, braised, or sautéed, its delicate yet fragrant aroma enhancing lots of meat, poultry,

and fish dishes. Incidentally, raw fennel is a popular dessert in Italy. Perhaps not to everyone's taste, but it is undoubtedly pure vitamin C. Then there are the seeds, whose essential oil exudes a wonderful fragrance of ani-seed. When boiled and drunk as tea, fennel seeds can relieve many a digestive problem.

SESAME
INFO

Sesame, probably the world's oldest oil plant, grows in the tropics. The seeds, which are available in yellow, black, and red, are encased in a capsule that is difficult to open when still unripe. But that is when

the seeds are at their most nutritious. They are roasted, their nutty aroma making them a popular ingredient in lots of main dishes, salads, and soups, and in both spicy and sweet recipes. They are the main ingredient in the popular flavoring paste of Middle Eastern cuisine, tahini.

Serves 4

4	*fennel*
2 tbsp	*olive oil*
3 tbsp	*white wine*
generous ³/₄ cup (200 ml)	*vegetable bouillon*
3 tbsp	*sesame seeds*
¹/₄ bunch	*parsley, chopped*

Step by step

Trim the fennel and remove the outer layers.

Pour over the white wine. Add the vegetable bouillon.

Cut each fennel into four, slice, then finely chop the green leaves.

Cover and simmer for about 35 minutes, until the fennel is al dente.

Sauté the sliced fennel in olive oil in a pan.

Toast the sesame seeds in a skillet. Sprinkle over the fennel with the green tops and parsley.

FENNEL
braised with toasted sesame

FENNEL
several variations

Did you know that fennel is a typical Italian vegetable? Its Italian name is "finocchio," and the Italians like to eat it raw or cold. But we think it tastes even better braised, sautéed, fried, grilled, or au gratin.

... au gratin, with potatoes, carrots, and pears

Combine $^2/_3$ cup (150 ml) light cream, 10 tablespoons (150 g) crème fraîche, and $3^1/_2$ oz (100 g) cream cheese, and season with salt and pepper. Slice generous 1 lb (500 g) peeled potatoes, 9 oz (250 g) carrots, and 4 sliced fennel in a gratin dish. Add 2 peeled, diced pears. Pour over the cream mixture and sprinkle with scant 1 cup (100 g) grated Gouda. Bake at 400 °F/200 °C for about 40 minutes.

... preserved in chile and served as antipasti

Deseed and finely chop 2 chiles. Combine with 6 tablespoons olive oil, 3 tablespoons lemon juice, and 1 tablespoon white wine vinegar. Season with salt and pepper. Chop 2 tablespoons each fresh basil, thyme, and marjoram, and stir into the marinade. Pour over boiled fennel, and leave to stand for about four hours. Serve cold, with toasted white bread.

... Italian style

Cook $1^1/_4$ lb (600 g) fennel, cut in half, in boiling salt water. Drain. Sauté 2 chopped onions in olive oil. Add 1 sliced red chile, $5^1/_2$ oz (150 g) soaked and chopped bolete, and 9 oz (250 g) skinned, chopped tomatoes, and continue cooking. Season with chopped parsley, 1 teaspoon freshly chopped thyme, and fennel seeds. Pour over $^1/_2$ cup (125 ml) white wine. Simmer gently for 5 minutes. Serve cold, with fresh bread.

... au gratin

Blanch 4 fennel cut in half in $^1/_2$ cup (125 ml) each white wine and bouillon, and season with salt and nutmeg. Remove, and layer in a greased ovenproof dish. Bind the cooking juices with cornstarch and fold in 3 tablespoons chopped parsley. Pour over the sliced fennel. Sprinkle with $2^1/_2$ oz (75 g) grated Parmesan. Bake at 425 F/220 °C for 30 minutes.

SAUCES
for fennel

Whether with or without meat, fennel is delicious with any of these sauces.

Cured ham sauce

Make a roux from butter and flour, and thin with fennel cooking juices. Stir in half-and-half cream. Season with salt and pepper, and fold in some thinly sliced cured ham. Goes well with braised and roasted fennel.

Rémoulade sauce

Mix together mayonnaise, yogurt, chopped gherkin and capers, 1 chopped hard-boiled egg, salt, and pepper. Goes well with fennel skewers.

Herb butter sauce

Sauté a chopped onion, dandelion, wild garlic, and water-cress in herb butter. Pour over some vegetable bouillon. Reduce slightly. Goes well with baked fennel and makes an excellent filling.

... as skewers with bell pepper and mushrooms

Trim 16 mushrooms. Alternate 4 fennel, cooked and cut in half, 4 large red bell peppers cut into large pieces, and the mushrooms on soaked wooden skewers. Combine 2 tablespoons each chopped parsley and chives with 4 tablespoons olive oil, salt, and pepper, and brush over the skewers. Wrap in aluminum foil and grill or roast in the oven at 425 °F/220 °C for 35 minutes.

... with ground meat

Blanch and halve 4 fennel bulbs, and scoop out some flesh from the centers. Combine this with 14 oz (400 g) ground meat, 1 teaspoon chopped sage, salt, pepper, and 6 tablespoons (100 g) crème fraîche. Spoon into the fennel halves. Place in a gratin dish. Pour over ½ cup (125 ml) each wine and vegetable bouillon, and bake in the oven at 325 °F/160 °C for 25 minutes. Sprinkle over chopped fennel leaves.

CARROTS
glazed with parsley

INFO

The first **baby carrots** really do taste best just sautéed in a little butter. This makes the most of their delicate, sugary aroma. They contain at least 5 percent sugar, and always need butter or oil. That's because they contain beta-carotene, which our bodies cannot process into vitamin A without fat. If you are drinking a glass of freshly pressed orange juice, remember to add a few drops of olive oil.

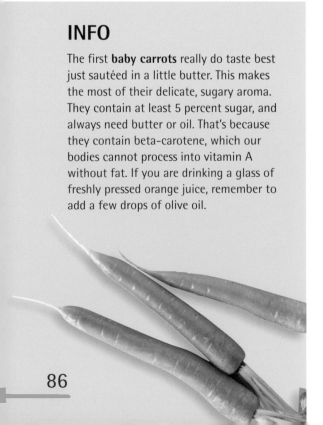

Serves 4

1³/₄ lb (750 g)	*baby carrots*
3 tbsp	*butter*
2	*onions, chopped*
1 cup (250 ml)	*vegetable bouillon*
	Salt
	Pepper
¹/₂ tsp	*sugar*
¹/₂ bunch	*parsley, chopped*

Step by step

Wash the carrots, and cut the green leaves off just above the carrot tops.

Melt the butter in a pan. Sweat the onions until transparent.

Add the carrots to the onions, and coat them in the fat.

Pour over the bouillon and simmer for 15–20 minutes until the liquid has been absorbed.

Season the carrots with salt, pepper, and sugar, and sprinkle over the parsley before serving.

Side dish

Roast veal with pepper and caper sauce: rub salt, pepper, and ground paprika into a veal joint weighing 1³/₄ lb (800 g). Heat 3 tablespoons clarified butter and fry the joint on all sides for 5 minutes. Deglaze the pan with 3 tablespoons brandy and ¹/₂ cup (125 ml) each meat bouillon and white wine. Simmer gently for about 1¹/₂ hours. Remove the meat, then bring the cooking juices to a boil. Reduce, and stir in 2 tablespoons capers and 1 tablespoon crushed pink peppercorns.

Side dish

Braised duck legs: trim any excess fat from 4 duck legs with skin, and rub with salt and pepper. Heat 3 tablespoons oil in a skillet and fry the legs, skin side down, for 3–4 minutes. Turn, and fry on the other side for 3 minutes. Pour over 2 cups (500 ml) bouillon and simmer the legs over low heat for 1 hour 10 minutes, turning once.

SIDE DISHES
for carrots

Combine cooked or glazed carrots with one of these side dishes for a complete meal.

Barley and asparagus risotto

Sauté chopped shallots in oil. Add some pearl parley and pour over wine and bouillon. Simmer until soft. Add chopped asparagus just before the end of the cooking time. Stir in butter and Parmesan to serve.

Broccoli couscous

Sweat broccoli rosettes in butter. Stir in 1 cup (200 g) couscous. Add vegetable bouillon, and leave to absorb. Season with salt and pepper, and fold in butter.

Cilantro rice

Sweat 1¼ cups (250 g) long-grain rice. Add double the quantity of water. Season with salt, and cook until just done. Stir in 3 tablespoons freshly chopped cilantro.

CARROTS
several

Young carrots in bunches need only be cleaned under running water with a vegetable brush. There is no need to peel them, because the skins are still very thin. As with most vegetables, the skins contain lots of minerals and vitamins. If you buy organic carrots, you can be sure that neither the

... with rice noodles and leeks

Pour hot water over 11 oz (300 g) rice noodles, and leave to absorb. Thinly slice 7 oz (200 g) young carrots diagonally, and cut 9 oz (250 g) leeks into strips. Sauté both in 3 tablespoons peanut oil with 1 chopped garlic clove and 1 teaspoon grated ginger. Fold in the noodles, 2 tablespoons roasted peanuts, and 7 oz (200 g) fried beef strips. Season to taste with salt, pepper, and soy sauce.

... as soup with apricots and chile

Simmer generous 1 lb (500 g) sliced, young carrots in 1⅔ cups (400 ml) each chicken bouillon and water for 8 minutes. Add 9 oz (250 g) apricot halves, either fresh or canned. Add the juice and grated rind of 1 lime, 1 oz (30 g) freshly grated ginger, and 1 finely chopped chile, and purée. Season to taste with 1 teaspoon sugar, salt, and 3 tablespoons sherry. Sprinkle with 1¾ oz (50 g) chopped apricots and mint.

variations

skins nor the carrots themselves contain any harmful substances. The four following versions offer suggestions for carrots Asian style, au gratin, as a soup, and glazed with sugar.

... au gratin, with fennel and turkey breast

Sauté 1 sliced onion in oil. Add 1³/₄ lb (750 g) young carrots, cut into quarters, and 11 oz (300 g) fennel cut into strips, and simmer. Pour over 1 cup (250 ml) vegetable bouillon and 7 tablespoons (100 ml) light cream, and cook until soft. Season with salt and pepper. Put the vegetables in an ovenproof dish. Add 5¹/₂ oz (150 g) smoked turkey breast cut into strips, and sprinkle with scant 1 cup (100 g) grated Emmental. Bake at 400 °F/200 °C for 20 minutes.

... glazed, with sesame seeds

Trim 1³/₄ lb (750 g) carrots and cut off the green leaves. Cut any larger carrots into two. Sauté in a pan in 3 tablespoons butter. Sprinkle over 3¹/₂ tablespoons (50 g) sugar and stir until it has dissolved. Add 1 cup (250 ml) bouillon. Season with salt and pepper, and simmer uncovered until the liquid has evaporated and the carrots are glazed. Sprinkle with toasted sesame seeds.

SAUCES
for carrots

These three sauces make perfect complements to the carrots and rice, risotto, and couscous recipe variations.

Ginger sauce

Sauté a chopped onion with garlic. Dust with flour, then add bouillon and light cream. Simmer until smooth. Season with salt and pepper, and stir in a piece of chopped preserved ginger.

Orange sauce

Make a roux, add bouillon and light cream, and stir until smooth. Fold in the juice and grated rind of 1 organic orange. Season to taste with orange liqueur.

Chervil and caper sauce

Sauté sliced leeks in butter. Dust with flour, then add bouillon and light cream. Stir until smooth, and fold in chopped chervil, capers, and mixed peppercorns.

FALL

Fall is when delicious vegetables such as leeks, pumpkins, celeriac, salsify, various cabbages, and beet come into season. And the woods and forest are full of mushrooms, such as chanterelles.

Join us in celebrating harvest at home with lots of recipes and countless variations from all over the world.

LEEKS
in a white sauce

Serves 4

1 3/4 lb (800 g)	leeks
4 tbsp	butter
3 tbsp	flour
2/3 cup (150 ml)	vegetable bouillon
7 tbsp (100 ml)	light cream
	Salt
	Pepper
	Freshly grated nutmeg

Step by step

Wash the leeks thoroughly, and slice the white and green sections into rings.

Sprinkle the flour over the butter when it is hot and foaming, and stir in.

Cook the sliced leeks in boiling salt water for 10 minutes.

Add the bouillon and bring to a boil, stirring continuously.

Start the sauce by melting the butter in a pan.

Add the cream, then season with salt and pepper. Stir the leeks into the sauce and grate over the nutmeg.

LEEKS INFO

The **leek** is a bulbous plant, and related to garlic and onions—which becomes obvious as soon you start to use it. Although it doesn't necessarily bring tears to your eyes, it is quite pungent. Its

strong aroma adds flavor, not only to soups and stews, but also to vegetable and meat dishes, and is excellent in pies and quiches.
The harvest starts in August. Winter leeks are available until February or March. The health-conscious know that leeks contain lots of minerals, such as iron and calcium, and that they are low in calories.

CORIANDER AND CILANTRO INFO

Most of us are familiar with **cilantro**, the green leafy herb, also

called Chinese parsley by aficionados, and **coriander**, the seeds of an umbelliferous plant that is used as a seasoning in cooking and baking. With regard to the flavor/aroma of the green herb, opinion is most definitely divided. Some people think it tastes of soap, while others swear by its lemony-pepperiness that is found in many oriental and Asian dishes. The green herb is called coriander in Europe, and cilantro in the USA.

LEEKS
several variations

Leeks are extremely versatile. As well as being very healthy and low in calories, they can also be used in many different ways. We give you six recipe variations for leek dishes here.

... as curry with zucchini, coconut milk, and chile

Sweat 7 oz (200 g) sliced leeks in 1 tablespoon oil. Add 1 chopped chile and 9 oz (250 g) thinly sliced zucchini, and sprinkle 3 teaspoons curry powder over the top. Add generous $^3/_4$ cup (200 ml) vegetable bouillon, and reduce by one-third. Pour in 7 tablespoons (100 ml) coconut milk. Bring to a boil, and season with salt and pepper.

... as lasagna with four cheeses

Alternate 12 sheets ready to cook lasagna with cooked leeks (see previous page) in an ovenproof dish. Finish with a layer of leeks. Sprinkle roasted sunflower seeds over each layer. Top each layer alternately with sliced mozzarella, chopped Feta, goat's cheese, and grated Emmental. Bake at 400 °F/200 °C for 45 minutes.

... as tagliatelle, with carrots, and chicken breasts

Cook 14 oz (400 g) tagliatelle until al dente. Sweat 7 oz (200 g) sliced leeks with 5$^1/_2$ oz (150 g) diced chicken breasts. Add 9 oz (250 g) each diced celeriac and carrots. Pour in 1 lb (450 g) canned tomatoes with their juice, and simmer for 10 minutes. Season with salt and pepper, and stir in chopped basil. Fold in the drained pasta. Sprinkle over grated Parmesan if desired.

... as a filling for stuffed potatoes

Boil 8 large potatoes in their skins in salt water, until just turning soft. Drain, and rub salt into the skins. Halve the potatoes and scoop out the flesh, leaving a rim of about $^1/_2$ in. (1 cm). Dry fry 10 tablespoons (80 g) pine nuts. Stir into the leeks (see previous page for preparation), and spoon into the potato halves. Sprinkle with grated Cheddar. Bake at 425 °F/220 °C for about 25 minutes.

SAUCES AND DIPS
for leeks

Leeks go equally well with spicy dips and creamy sauces.

Blue cheese dip
Combine blue cheese with creamed cottage cheese, milk, and mayonnaise. Goes well with leek tart.

Tomato and paprika dip
Combine crème fraîche with lemon juice, tomato paste, ground paprika, salt, and pepper. Goes well with stuffed potatoes.

Cilantro and pimento sauce
Make a roux, and stir to a creamy sauce with chicken bouillon. Season with pimento, nutmeg, lemon juice, salt, and pepper. Stir in chopped parsley and cilantro. Goes well with cooked leeks.

... as soup, with potatoes, and sausages
Sweat 14 oz (400 g) sliced leeks in 2 tablespoons oil. Add 14 oz (400 g) diced, peeled potatoes to 4 cups (1 liter) vegetable bouillon and cook for 30 minutes. Pour in 7 tablespoons (100 ml) light cream and season with salt, pepper, and nutmeg. Slice 4 frankfurters (or other smoked sausage) and heat in the broth. Sprinkle with chopped parsley and 1 tablespoon each chopped thyme and marjoram.

... as a tart, with apples, and nuts
Make pastry from 1$\frac{1}{3}$ cups (200 g) all-purpose flour, 7 tablespoons (100 g) butter, 1 egg, and a pinch of salt. Knead, and leave to rest for 30 minutes. Roll out and use to line a greased tart pan. Sweat 7 oz (200 g) each diced apple and sliced leeks in 1 tablespoon butter, and add generous $\frac{3}{4}$ cup (100 g) chopped walnuts. Pour into the tart shell. Combine generous $\frac{3}{4}$ cup (200 g) crème fraîche with 1 egg, salt, and pepper, and pour over the leek mixture. Bake at 400 °F/200 °C for 40 minutes.

CORN
INFO

The edible part of the **corn plant**—whose presence in Europe is thanks to Christopher Columbus—are the cobs, which are made up of hundreds of tiny yellow kernels. Each plant grows

about 2–3 cobs, each one wrapped in a tough, fibrous sheath. The cobs can be boiled, fried, or barbecued, then served (and eaten) whole; or the kernels removed and consumed decorously with a fork. Sweet corn is the tastiest variety. Eaten as a vegetable when young, corn is also ground into cornmeal, which is widely used in baking and to make polenta, among other dishes; and more finely ground into cornstarch, used as a binder in cooking. The Mexicans use corn to brew beer and make spirits. Among the best known corn products are the breakfast cereal, corn flakes, and popcorn—essential for the movies. Finally, let's not forget corn oil, which is high in polyunsaturates, including the essential fatty acid, linolenic acid.

CHIVES
INFO

Chives grow in bundles, which is to say 4 or 5 thin stalks grow

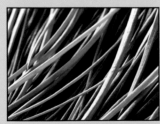

from each tiny bulb. They are cut just above ground level; the stalks quickly grow again. The flower is edible.

96

Serves 4

8	whole corn cobs, halved
	Salt
²/₃ cup (150 g)	butter
1 bunch	parsley, chopped
1 bunch	chives, sliced
1 bunch	dill, chopped
3¹/₂ oz (100 g)	cherry tomatoes
2	scallions, cut into rings

Step by step

Trim and wash the corn cobs, and boil in salt water for 30 minutes. Remove.

Halve the cherry tomatoes, and sweat briefly in the pan with the scallions.

Combine 7 tablespoons (100 g) of the butter with the herbs, and set aside.

Brush the herb butter over the corn on the cob.

Brush the remaining butter over the corn cobs and brown them in a skillet until crisp.

Serve with the cherry tomatoes and scallions.

CORN ON THE COB
with herb butter

SAUCES
for corn on the cob

The following sauces make the perfect companions for corn on the cob:

Herb and chile cream sauce
Combine sautéed scallions, light cream, and crème fraîche. Simmer, and season with salt and pepper. Stir in chopped herbs and chile. Goes well with sautéed and barbecued corn on the cob.

Tarragon and meat sauce
Brown ground beef and chopped onion in a pan. Stir in meat bouillon and tomato paste, and reduce the liquid. Season with chopped tarragon, salt, pepper, and ground paprika. Add gin to taste. Goes well with corn on the cob baked in foil or barbecued.

Shrimp sauce
Sweat chopped shallots, and add shrimp. Stir in meat bouillon, light cream, and tomato paste, and reduce by one-half. Season to taste with salt, pepper, and dill. Goes well with patties, and barbecued corn on the cob.

CORN ON THE COB
several

The delicious, yellow cobs taste best fresh, with a little butter. Below are some variations for you to try. However, in case you find this too boring, in some, the cobs are used whole, in others they are cut into slices, and in others only the kernels are used. Of course, if you are in a hurry, you can

... with bell peppers, mushrooms, and onions
Make a marinade from 6 tablespoons olive oil, 2 tablespoons vinegar, $\frac{1}{4}$ teaspoon cayenne, $\frac{1}{4}$ teaspoon ground paprika, salt, and pepper. Cut 1 red and 1 yellow bell pepper into large pieces. On skewers, alternate the chunks of bell pepper, cooked, sliced corn, 5 $\frac{1}{2}$ oz (150 g) mushrooms, and onions cut into eighths, and marinate for 45 minutes. Fry, grill, or barbecue until crisp.

... cooked in foil, with wine and herbs
Soak the corn in white wine for about 30 minutes. Brush with oil, without draining. Wrap each corn cob in aluminum foil with a few herb sprigs, and bake in the oven at 425 °F/220 °C for about 45 minutes.

variations

use pre-cooked cobs or canned sweet corn kernels. They go well in spicy, creamy sauces, and fresh dips.

... as patties with carrots and wheat

Sweat 3 sliced scallions in butter for a few moments. Pour over 1¼ cups (300 ml) vegetable bouillon. Add 1¼ cups (200 g) wheat flour, and simmer for 15 minutes. Grate 9 oz (250 g) carrots, and add to the pan with 1¾ lb (800 g) cooked sweet corn. Season with salt and pepper. Shape into patties and fry each side in oil for 5 minutes, until crisp.

... as quick and easy soup

Sweat 2 chopped onions in butter until transparent. Pour over 4 cups (1 liter) vegetable bouillon. Skin and finely chop 6 tomatoes. Add to the pan with 1¾ lb (800 g) sweetcorn, and simmer for 10 minutes. Whisk with a handheld blender until creamy. Stir in ⅔ cup (100 ml) light cream. Season with salt and pepper. Sprinkle over 2 tablespoons each thyme and parsley.

DIPS
for corn on the cob

These three refreshing dips are perfect with freshly grilled or barbecued corn on the cob. They don't take long to make.

Salmon dip

Combine quark, mayonnaise, mustard, and freshly chopped herbs, and season with salt and pepper. Fold in freshly chopped salmon. Goes well with grilled corn on the cob.

Avocado dip

Blend together puréed avocado, sour cream, chile oil, and lemon juice. Season with salt and pepper.

Cheese spread dip

Blend together sour cream, cheese spread, pepper, ground paprika, and nutmeg. Stir in some chopped chives.

CELERIAC
w i t h   a   c h e e s e   c o a t i n g

Serves 4

generous 1 lb (500 g)	*celeriac*
	Salt
1 tbsp	*lemon juice*
	Pepper
²/₃ cup (100 g)	*flour*
2	*eggs*
4 tbsp	*dried breadcrumbs*
4 tbsp	*freshly grated pecorino*
generous ³/₄ cup (200 ml)	*cooking oil*

INFO

You can tell how fresh **celeriac** is by testing how firm and heavy it is. If it sounds hollow when you tap it, it is old, and the flesh will be fibrous and flaccid. Small tubers are the tastiest. Raw celeriac will keep in the icebox for about 5 days. Once cut, it should be wrapped in aluminum foil and used quickly.

Step by step

Peel the celeriac, then halve and cut it into slices ¹/₂-in. (1-cm) thick.

Cook the celeriac slices in boiling salt water and lemon juice for 12 minutes.

Drain, pat dry, and season with salt and pepper.

Put the flour, beaten eggs, and breadcrumbs mixed with the pecorino in 3 separate dishes.

Coat the celeriac slices, first in flour, then egg, then breadcrumbs. Shake gently to remove any excess.

Heat the oil, and fry the slices until golden.

INFO

A homemade **rémoulade sauce** is the perfect dip for celeriac schnitzel and potato chips. Stir 7 tablespoons mayonnaise, 5 oz (150 g) yogurt, and 1 teaspoon mustard together until creamy. Finely chop 3 cornichons. Chop 2 tablespoons capers. Finely chop 1 bunch each chives and parsley, and combine with the yogurt and mayonnaise mix. Season to taste with salt, pepper, and sugar.

Side dish

Try homemade **potato chips** with baked celeriac schnitzels. Wash, peel, and halve 4 large potatoes and slice thinly, ideally using a mandoline. Pat dry. Fry in hot oil until crispy. Drain on paper towels, and season with salt.

SIDE DISHES
for celeriac

Eggs, other vegetables, and potatoes all go well with celeriac.

Stuffed eggs

Hard-boil some eggs. Peel, then halve them, and scoop out the yolks. Combine with mustard, mayonnaise, and chopped chives. Pipe into the egg halves with a pastry bag. Goes well with celeriac schnitzel, and purée.

Fried potato sticks

Peel some potatoes. Cut them into matchstick-size pieces, and fry in hot oil until crispy. Goes well with celeriac au gratin, purée, and studded celeriac.

Carrots in Marsala

Thinly slice the carrots. Sweat in a pan with 1 chopped shallot. Add Marsala, the carrots, and simmer gently. Season to taste. Goes well with celeriac purée and schnitzel, and studded celeriac.

CELERIAC
several

This large tuber is irregularly shaped and certainly no beauty, but the interior appeals for its unmistakable flavor and healthy nutrients. Celeriac used to be best known as one of the ingredients used for soup. It can, however, also be prepared in lots of other delicious ways. Try it as celeriac purée, studded

... as a purée

Chop $1^3/_4$ lb (800 g) celeriac into small pieces. Cook in boiling water with 1 tablespoon lemon juice and salt for 20 minutes. Drain through a dishtowel, and squeeze out well. Purée in a blender with 14 tablespoons (200 g) cold butter, salt, pepper, nutmeg, and 1 tablespoon lemon juice. Garnish with fried parsley.

... au gratin, with sauce Mornay

Cook 14 oz (400 g) sliced celeriac in boiling water for 5 minutes. Drain, and place the slices in an ovenproof dish. Make a roux, and thin with 1 cup (250 ml) each milk and light cream. Season with salt, pepper, lemon, Tabasco® Sauce, and nutmeg. Stir in 7 tablespoons (50 g) freshly grated Parmesan. Sprinkle 7 tablespoons (50 g) Gruyère over the celeriac. Bake at 400 °F/200 °C for 20 minutes.

SAUCES
for celeriac

Horseradish and curry go beautifully with this tasty root. Try these sauces:

Horseradish sauce
Sweat chopped onion in butter. Stir in some flour and make into a sauce with vegetable bouillon and light cream. Add freshly grated horseradish and blend. Season with salt and pepper, and fold in some chopped chives.

Curry and almond sauce
Make a roux from butter and flour. Add milk and white wine to make a sauce. Add salt, pepper, and curry powder. Fold in ground almonds. Goes well with studded celeriac, and celeriac schnitzels.

Curry and orange sauce
Sauté chopped shallots and grated ginger, and dust with flour. Deglaze the pan with bouillon and orange juice. Add sherry and lemon juice, and reduce by one-third. Season with salt, pepper, and curry powder.

---

variations

slices, au gratin, or as a vegetable with apples. Add a few drops of lemon juice to the cooking water to prevent it from discoloring, or plunge it into cold lemon water.

... studded with ham and sage
Peel 1 celeriac and cut into 12 slices. Cut 2 openings in the top of each slice. Insert $^1/_4$ slice boiled ham and 1 sage leaf into each opening. Heat 3 tablespoons clarified butter, and carefully brown the celeriac slices on all sides. Season with salt and pepper. Add $^2/_3$ cup (150 ml) vegetable bouillon, and cook for a further 5 minutes.

... as a vegetable, with apples
Peel celeriac and apple, and cut into slices or pieces. Sprinkle with lemon juice. Bring apple juice to a boil with lemon and salt. Cook the celeriac first for 5 minutes, then the apple. Remove from the pan. Reduce the cooking juices, and bind with cold butter. Serve with the vegetables, sprinkled with chopped chives.

BEET INFO

What is remarkable about this apparently unassuming root is its intensely red color, which dyes the hands when working with it. In fact, the dye is often used in industry for coloring confectionery, ice cream, jams, and jellies. Botanically, it is a turnip;

it is also known as garden beet, red beet, and, particularly in Great Britain, beetroot. Turnips generally pack quite a punch: they boost the immune system, and are antibacterial. **Beet** goes well with braised beef, lamb, and game; fried or grilled sausages and hamburgers; and fish and pasta dishes.

BOUQUET GARNI INFO

A **bouquet garni** is a bunch of mixed herbs that is used to flavor soups, broths, and sauces. It is removed at the end of cooking. Depending on the particular dish, it can be made

with parsley, bay leaves, thyme, and rosemary, but also tarragon, savory, and marjoram. Instead of tying them into a bouquet, the herbs can also be put inside a little muslin bag and added to the pot.

Serves 4

1³/₄ lb (800 g)	beet
2	red onions, diced
1 large	russet apple, peeled, cored, and chopped
2 tbsp	lard
¹/₂ cup (120 ml)	port
¹/₂ cup (120 ml)	vegetable bouillon
1	bouquet garni (parsley, thyme, bay leaf)
	Salt, white pepper
1 pinch	ground cumin
1 pinch	sugar
	Apple juice
2 tbsp	crème fraîche

Step by step

Scrub the beet well. Do not remove the stalks, as otherwise the beet will "bleed." Cook the beet.

Add the port, vegetable bouillon, and bouquet garni. Season with salt, pepper, and cumin. Cook for 20 minutes until al dente.

Allow the beet to cool, peel (wearing kitchen gloves), then cut into short sticks, ¹/₂-in. (1–cm) thick.

Stir in the beet, and season with the sugar and apple juice.

Sauté the onions and diced apple in the lard.

Stir in the crème fraîche to finish.

BEET
with onions and apple

SAUCES
for beet

These three sauces harmonize beautifully with the slightly earthy flavor of beet.

Pesto sauce
Make a béchamel sauce from butter, flour, milk, and bouillon. Season with basil pesto and Parmesan.

Sage sauce
Make a béchamel sauce from butter, flour, milk, and bouillon. Finish with freshly chopped sage leaves and ground pimento.

Tomato and pear sauce
Make a creamy tomato sauce from puréed tomatoes and a little bouillon. Fold in some diced pears. Garnish with chives.

BEET
several

Beets "bleed" quite dramatically, and will quickly turn any dish a strong red color. If they are prepared separately, they should be cooked first, then peeled, and chopped or diced, as otherwise all the color will run into the cooking water. Most of us are familiar with beet that has been preserved in vinegar and

... vegetable tart with cheese
Make a short pastry dough and use it to line a tart pan. Combine 1³/₄ lb (800 g) coarsely grated beets, 4 chopped onions, 2 chopped garlic cloves, ¹/₄ teaspoon coriander, and 2 tablespoons bread-crumbs, and smooth over the pastry. Whisk together 1 egg yolk and ¹/₂ cup (120 ml) milk, scant 1 cup (100 g) grated pecorino, 1 whisked egg white, pepper, and salt, and spoon over the beet mixture. Bake at 350 °F/180 °C for 45 minutes.

... stuffed with lamb and bulgur
Scoop out 4 large, cooked beet. Combine 7 oz (200 g) ground lamb, 3¹/₂ oz (100 g) cooked bulgur, 1 egg, 1 chopped chile, 1 chopped garlic clove, 1 tablespoon tomato paste, salt, and pepper. Spoon into the beet. Wrap them in aluminum foil and bake at 350 °F/180 °C for 40 minutes. Crumble over some Feta and bake at 400 °F/200 °C.

variations

is used to add color to salads. But have you ever tried beet in a pasta sauce? Or au gratin, with apple and horseradish? Stuffed with bulgur and lamb? Let us surprise you with some completely new taste experiences!

... au gratin, with horseradish and apples

Peel 1³/₄ lb (800 g) beet, 2 apples, and 2 carrots, then cut into thin slices and layer in an ovenproof dish. Pour over a sauce of generous ³/₄ cup (200 g) crème fraîche, 2 eggs, 2 tablespoons grated horseradish, salt, pepper, ground pimento, and cumin. Bake at 350 °F/180 °C for 30 minutes. Sprinkle with grated Cheddar to serve.

... preserved in vinegar and spices

Slice generous 1 lb (500 g) cooked beet. Bring 1 cup (250 ml) red wine vinegar, 1 roughly chopped onion, 6 each peppercorns and pimento berries, 2 cloves, 2 bay leaves, and 1 teaspoon grated lemon rind to a boil. Add the beet and simmer for 5 minutes. Chill in the icebox for at least 12 hours.

DIPS
for beet

Three sauces for beet—one fruity, one with cheese, and one a horseradish dip. Try and choose a favorite!

Sweet and sour sauce

Bring apricot juice, chopped mango, the juice and grated rind of 1 lime, turmeric, chopped cilantro, chopped pistachios, and light cream to a boil, then reduce by one-third. Goes well with preserved beet.

Cheese sauce

Combine flour and butter. Stir in white wine and meat bouillon. Add grated cheese. Season to taste with salt and pepper. Goes well with beet au gratin, and stuffed beet.

Horseradish dip

Soak a stale roll in vegetable bouillon, crumble, and heat in a pan. Blend with freshly grated horseradish and season with salt, pepper, and sugar. Stir in some butter. Goes well with the au gratin, and vegetable tart recipe variations.

SQUASH
with coconut milk and cilantro

SQUASH/PUMPKIN INFO

It's hard to imagine fall without the type of **Winter squash** called **pumpkin**. The different varieties are available in a tremendous range of colors and are not just useful in cooking—as seen at Halloween, for example, pumpkins can be carved into intricate shapes and used as lanterns. The flesh of the pumpkin is excellent in soups, as a vegetable, puréed, preserved, and stuffed. Pumpkin seeds are also highly nutritious, and are thought to have medicinal properties. With

Summer squash varieties, the skin is thin, and can be eaten as well as the flesh. Their season runs from April through September.

Serves 4

1	medium-size summer squash (about 2$^{1}/_{4}$ lb/1 kg)
1	onion, chopped
3 tbsp	olive oil
	Salt
$^{1}/_{4}$ tsp	cayenne
$^{3}/_{4}$ cup (200 ml)	vegetable bouillon
$^{3}/_{4}$ cup (200 ml)	coconut milk
	Pepper
	Nutmeg
$^{1}/_{4}$ tsp	chile flakes
1 bunch	cilantro, chopped

Step by step

Halve and deseed the squash, then chop into small pieces. The skin will disintegrate during cooking.

Sauté the chopped onion in a little hot olive oil.

Add the squash and cook briefly. Season to taste with salt and cayenne.

Deglaze the pan with the bouillon and coconut milk, and cook for about 15 minutes until the squash is soft.

Season the squash to taste with salt, pepper, nutmeg, and the chile flakes. Sprinkle with cilantro to serve.

Side dish

Poached fish fillets go well with cooked pumpkin or squash. Wash and pat dry 4 fish fillets (about 7 oz/200 g each), e.g. pollock, cod, r salmon. Depending on the variety, poach the fish in a little water for 7–10 minutes. Season with salt and pepper. The fish fillets can be placed on the pumpkin for the last 10 minutes of the cooking time.

Side dish

Raisin rice goes very well with pumpkin and fish. Sweat 1 cup (200 g) rice and 1 chopped onion in a little oil. Pour over $1^2/_3$ cups (400 ml) vegetable bouillon. Cook the rice for 15–20 minutes. Stir in 6 tablespoons (50 g) raisins. Season with salt and pepper.

SAUCES AND DIPS
for squash or pumpkin

Three unusual sauces to go with at least one of the recipe variations.

Walnut and crème fraîche
Stir together crème fraîche, milk, light cream, 7 tablespoons (50 g) roasted, chopped walnuts, salt, pepper, and nutmeg. Goes well with the quiche, and au gratin variations.

Spicy tomato sauce
Make a smooth sauce from canned tomatoes, chopped onion, and chopped chile. Season well with salt, pepper, thyme, and Tabasco® Sauce. Goes well with stuffed pumpkin.

Mango and pistachio sauce
Make a roux, add bouillon and light cream, and reduce by one-half. Sweat mango flesh with the juice and rind of 1 lime, season with turmeric, and stir into the cream sauce with chopped pistachios. Goes well with the vegetables and noodles variations.

... as cream soup, with carrots, and sesame seed oil
Dice generous 1 lb (500 g) pumpkin or squash, 7 oz (200 g) carrots, 1 onion, and 2 potatoes, and cook in $3\frac{1}{4}$ cups (750 ml) bouillon for about 15 minutes. Purée. Stir in 7 tablespoons (100 ml) light cream. Season to taste with salt, pepper, and nutmeg. Top with a spoon of whisked light whipping cream before serving. Drizzle over a few drops of sesame seed oil.

... as an ingredient in pasta dough
Knead together scant $3\frac{1}{2}$ cups (500 g) wheat flour with 6 oz (175 g) pumpkin or squash purée, 1 tablespoon sesame seed oil, salt, and pepper. Wrap in aluminum foil and chill for 30 minutes. Roll the pasta dough out very thinly, then cut into long strips. Cook the pasta in salt water.

SQUASH/PUMPKIN
several variations

There are over 800 different varieties of pumpkin and squash in the world, and they all taste different. It's worth trying several out to find out which type you like best. Butternut squash, for example, is highly aromatic with a sweet, nutty flavor, while the shape and bland taste of marrow squash make it ideal for savory stuffing.

... as quiche, with walnuts, and crème fraîche

Knead together 1¹/₃ cups (200 g) flour, 7 tablespoons (100 g) butter, 2 eggs, and salt to make a dough. Wrap in aluminum foil and chill for 30 minutes. Roll out, then press into a greased quiche dish. Combine 9 oz (250 g) diced, cooked chicken breast, 3 diced tomatoes, 7 tablespoons (50 g) chopped walnuts, ¹/₂ cup (125 g) crème fraîche, salt, and pepper. Spread over the pastry. Bake at 400 °C/200 °C for about 30 minutes. Garnish with basil.

... stewed with pork, potatoes, and chile

Dice 11 oz (300 g) pork loin, and simmer in bouillon for about 15 minutes. Peel and dice 6 potatoes and generous 1 lb (500 g) pumpkin or squash. Skin, deseed, and finely chop 2 tomatoes. Deseed and chop a chile. Add to the pork, and simmer for a further 20 minutes. Season with salt and pepper, and sprinkle with chopped parsley.

... stuffed with ground lamb, rice, and olives

Halve and deseed a pumpkin or squash. Brush with oil and bake at 425 °F/220 °C for 10 minutes. Sauté 14 oz (400 g) ground lamb in olive oil. Season with salt, pepper, and a little nutmeg. Cook 1 cup (200 g) long-grain rice in accordance with the pack instructions. Combine with the ground lamb and 1³/₄ oz (50 g) pitted, chopped olives and spoon into the pumpkin or squash. Cover with aluminum foil and bake for 15 minutes; then remove the foil and bake for a further 10 minutes.

... au gratin, with zucchini, and ginger

Thinly slice generous 1 lb (500 g) zucchini. Peel and grate 2 in. (5 cm) fresh ginger, and sweat with the zucchini and ³/₄ cup (100 g) sunflower seeds in 1 tablespoon oil. Layer the zucchini and sliced pumpkin or squash in an ovenproof dish, and sprinkle over 5¹/₂ oz (150 g) diced Feta. Bake at 400 F/200 °C for about 2-5 minutes.

CHANTERELLES
ragout with cream

Serves 4

1½ lb (700 g)	*chanterelles*
2 tbsp	*all-purpose flour*
2 tbsp	*butter*
3 oz (90 g)	*streaky bacon, diced*
3	*onions, diced*
2	*garlic cloves, finely chopped*
3 tbsp	*clarified butter*
	Salt
	Pepper
1 cup (250 ml)	*light cream*
1 cup (250 ml)	*chicken bouillon*
1 tbsp	*lemon juice*
1 bunch	*flat-leafed parsley, freshly chopped*

Step by step

Trim the chanterelles and dust with 1 tablespoon flour.

Pour over the cream and bouillon, and gradually stir in the roux.

Combine the butter with the remainder of the flour to make a roux. Stir well, then chill.

Simmer for 4 minutes, then season with salt, pepper, and lemon juice.

Sauté the bacon, onions, garlic, and chanterelles in hot clarified butter, then season with salt and pepper.

Stir the parsley into the ragout.

MUSHROOMS INFO

The **chanterelle** is easy to identify by its unmistakable trumpet shape: the stem is topped by a ruffle-edged cap with gills. The cap is usually yellow, which is why this delicate

mushroom is also known as the golden chanterelle. It is not cultivated commercially, but grows wild from June through October, preferring mossy coniferous and beech forests. It is chock-full of potassium! However, mushrooms also store harmful substances that accumulate in the ground, so it is not advisable to eat fresh mushrooms too often. When buying, look out for the smaller chanterelles, as they have a firmer consistency and are more aromatic. They are best sweated slowly in their own juices. Of course, Fall brings other mushrooms as well as chanterelles. In damp weather, you will find bolete, parasol

mushrooms, oyster mushrooms, and common field mushrooms, to name but a few of the best known varieties. But unless you're absolutely sure of your mushrooms, it's better to stick to cultivated ones. You will have plenty of choice, and they are available throughout the year to help you create a wide range of fabulous dishes.

CHANTERELLES
several variations

Whichever version you try, please remember that chanterelles must be cooked at a very high temperature, so use clarified butter and oil, which become hotter than butter.

... in an omelet

Combine 9 oz (250 g) diced soft cheese with 10 tablespoons (150 g) crème fraîche. Stir in 4 egg yolks, and season with salt, pepper, and nutmeg. Fold in 4 beaten egg whites. Sauté 1 chopped onion in 2 tablespoons rapeseed oil. Add 7 oz (200 g) trimmed chanterelles. Remove. Cook 4 omelets from the egg mixture, and garnish with the chanterelles and chopped parsley.

... as a filling for ravioli

Make a dough from 2 cups (300 g) wheat flour, 2 eggs, 2 egg yolks, salt, and 4 tablespoons olive oil, and leave to rest. Sweat 7 oz (200 g) chanterelles and a chopped onion in oil. Cool, then combine with 3$\frac{1}{2}$ oz (100 g) cream cheese, $\frac{1}{4}$ cup (30 g) grated Parmesan, and 1 egg yolk, and season with salt and pepper. Roll out the pasta dough. Cut into squares. Top with the mushroom mixture, place two halves together, and pinch all round to secure. Cook for 5–7 minutes.

... au gratin, with artichoke hearts

Drain 5$\frac{1}{2}$ oz (150 g) artichoke hearts from a jar, and sweat with 5$\frac{1}{2}$ oz (150 g) blanched peas in 3 tablespoons butter. Transfer to an ovenproof dish. Sweat generous 1 lb (500 g) trimmed chanterelles and a chopped onion in oil, then season with salt and pepper. Add $\frac{2}{3}$ cup (150 ml) bouillon and 7 tablespoons (100 ml) light cream, and cook until creamy. Pour over the vegetables, then sprinkle with 7 tablespoons (50 g) grated Gruyère. Bake at 350 F/180 °C for 15 minutes.

... on pizza, with goat's cheese, and bacon

Make a dough from 2$\frac{1}{2}$ cups (350 g) strong flour, 1 teaspoon each dried yeast and coriander, 1 cup (250 ml) water, and 2 tablespoons olive oil. Allow to rise. Place on a greased baking sheet. Top with 10 tablespoons (150 g) crème fraîche, 1 finely chopped chile, 1 thinly sliced onion, 2$\frac{1}{2}$ oz (75 g) sliced ham or bacon, 5$\frac{1}{2}$ oz (150 g) chanterelles, chopped parsley, and 3$\frac{1}{2}$ oz (100 g) crumbled goat's cheese. Drizzle with oil. Bake at 450 °F/230 °C for 20 minutes.

SIDE DISHES
for chanterelles

If you like dumplings, why not try them with bacon or herbs, or fry them for a change?

Bacon dumplings

Make a dough for dumplings, and combine with dry-fried diced bacon and diced onions. Shape into dumplings and cook. Goes well with the ragout, and game recipe variations.

Herb dumplings

Make a dough for dumplings. Instead of the parsley, add 5 tablespoons freshly chopped mixed herbs and onions. Shape into dumplings and cook. Goes well with the ragout, and game variations.

Fried dumplings

Make a dough from generous 1 lb (500 g) potato purée, salt, nutmeg, crème fraîche, butter, and flour. Shape into dumplings, then coat in flour, beaten eggs, and dried breadcrumbs. Fry in hot oil. Goes well with chanterelles au gratin.

... in game ragout

Sweat $5^1/_2$ oz (150 g) each chopped onion, carrot, and celery with $2^1/_4$ lb (1 kg) cubed game in 4 tablespoons oil. Add salt, pepper, 1 bay leaf, 6 juniper berries, 2 cloves, 1 sprig thyme, and 1 tablespoon tomato paste. Simmer, then add 1 cup (250 ml) red wine. Reduce, then add $2^1/_2$ cups (600 ml) meat bouillon. Cook for 1 hour. Add 11 oz (300 g) sweated chanterelles 10 minutes before the end of the cooking time.

... in soup with potatoes

Sweat $1^3/_4$ lb (600 g) diced peeled potatoes, $3^1/_2$ oz (100 g) diced carrots, and $2^1/_2$ oz (75 g) diced celery stalks in 2 tablespoons oil. Add 2 cups (500 ml) vegetable bouillon, 1 bay leaf, salt, and pepper. Simmer gently for 20 minutes. Sweat 12 oz (350 g) trimmed chanterelles in 4 tablespoons oil. Season with salt and pepper and add to the soup. Simmer gently for 15 minutes. Bind with 2 egg yolks and 3 tablespoons light cream. Sprinkle with chopped parsley.

POINTED/GREEN CABBAGE
with golden breadcrumbs

Serves 4

2	onions, chopped
1 tbsp	olive oil
2¹/₄ lb (1 kg)	pointed cabbage
	Salt
	Pepper
3 tbsp	white wine
7 tbsp	vegetable bouillon
14 tbsp (200 g)	butter
6 cups (300 g)	breadcrumbs
1 bunch	parsley, chopped

INFO

The **pointed cabbage**, native to Europe, is instantly recognizable by its tapering shape and wonderful green leaves. It is the principal ingredient in the sauerkraut produced in Germany and is harvested from May through December. It has a subtle flavor when freshly prepared and is at its best when simply sweated in a little butter. It is simply delicious when stuffed. And some more good news: it contains a precursor to vitamin C, which is turned into genuine vitamin C when it is cooked. If it is difficult to obtain pointed cabbage, the recipe on this page and its following variations are equally delicious with any fresh, green cabbage.

Step by step

Sweat the onions in hot olive oil, stirring continuously, until transparent.

Cut the cabbage into strips about 1-in. (3-cm) thick. Add to the onions, and sweat briefly. Season with salt and pepper.

Pour over the white wine. Add the vegetable bouillon, and simmer for about 25 minutes.

Melt the butter in a pan and heat.

Add the breadcrumbs, and fry in the butter until golden brown.

Sprinkle the breadcrumbs over the cabbage to serve, and garnish with the parsley.

Side dish

Pork goes very well with this recipe for cabbage. Wash and pat dry generous 1 lb (500 g) pork loin, and fry on all sides in 2 tablespoons hot cooking oil with 2 chopped onions. Pour over $^1/_2$ cup (125 ml) each meat bouillon and white wine. Transfer to an ovenproof dish and bake at 400 °F/200 °C for 25 minutes. Wrap in aluminum foil and leave to rest for 4 minutes. Cut into slices. Bring the cooking juices to a boil. Season with salt and pepper, bind with butter if desired, and serve with the pork. Sprinkle with crushed red pepper.

SIDE DISHES
for pointed/green cabbage

Lots of recipes with cabbage go well with these potato side dishes.

Sweet potato purée

Sauté diced sweet potatoes with chopped onion and chile. Add bouillon, salt, pepper, and a pinch of cinnamon, and simmer. Drain and purée. Add a little of the cooking juices, and stir until smooth. Goes well with cabbage au gratin.

Duchess potatoes

Combine potato purée with butter, egg yolk, salt, pepper, and nutmeg. Use a pastry bag to pipe rosettes onto a greased baking sheet. Brush with whisked egg yolk, and bake at 425 °F/220 °C for 10 minutes. Goes well with roulades, and cabbage with meatballs.

Boiled potatoes

Peel and halve the potatoes, and cook in a little salt water for 20 minutes. Drain and cool until no longer steaming. Goes well with roulades.

... roulades, with ground veal, and anchovies

Knead together 1 softened bread roll, 1 chopped onion, generous 1 lb (500 g) ground veal, $1^3/_4$ oz (50 g) anchovy fillets, and 1 egg. Place about 3 tablespoons of this mixture onto a blanched cabbage leaf, and tie up with kitchen string. Fry the roulades in a little olive oil in a casserole. Then cook in vegetable bouillon for about 30 minutes.

... with ground paprika, shiitake, chile, and chicken

Dice generous 1 lb (500 g) chicken breast fillets, and sauté in oil until crispy. Season with salt and ground paprika. Finely chop 1 bell pepper and 1 chile, and add to the pan together with 11 oz (300 g) blanched cabbage. Add 10 soaked and sliced shiitake mushrooms. Pour over 7 tablespoons (100 ml) bouillon and 2 tablespoons soy sauce, and season with salt, pepper, and Chinese five-spice powder.

POINTED/GREEN CABBAGE
several variations

Pointed cabbage is quite delicate with a subtle flavor, and should always be prepared when fresh, as otherwise it becomes soft and tasteless. With our variations, you'll always have some excellent recipes to hand.

... as stew, with potatoes, carrots, and celery

Dice generous 1 lb (500 g) potatoes, 9 oz (250 g) carrots, 5¹/₂ oz (150 g) celery, and generous 1 lb (500 g) beef. Brown briefly in oil. Add 8 cups (2 liters) vegetable bouillon plus generous 1 lb (500 g) sliced cabbage, and simmer for about 25 minutes. Season with fresh or dried garden herbs, and nutmeg

... with chile, scallions, and meatballs

Trim and thinly slice 3 scallions and 1 small chile. Combine generous 1 lb (500 g) seasoned ground pork with the chile, and shape into small balls. Fry in oil in a skillet with the spring onions until crispy

... au gratin, with Gouda and mozzarella

Place generous 1 lb (500 g) braised cabbage in an ovenproof dish. Combine 2 eggs, 5¹/₂ oz (150 g) cream cheese with herbs, and scant 1 cup (100 g) grated Gouda. Season with salt and pepper, and spoon over the cabbage. Cover the cabbage with sliced mozzarella. Bake at 400 °F/200 °C for approx. 35 minutes.

... with ground meat and pasta

Cook generous 1 lb (500 g) rigatoni in accordance with the pack instructions. Finely chop 1 onion, and sweat briefly in oil. Add 1¹/₄ lb (600 g) ground meat, and brown. Finally, add generous 1 lb (500 g) braised cabbage, and simmer briefly.

EGGPLANT INFO

Like tomatoes and potatoes, the purple eggplant is a member of the nightshade family, and botanically is, in fact, a berry. Eggplant contain solanin, which

is toxic, so they should not be eaten raw (neither should tomatoes, when they are still green). **Eggplant** is available in various shapes, sizes, and colors, including purple, white, green and orange. They are essential in ratatouille, the Mediterranean vegetable dish with tomatoes, zucchini, and bell peppers, and in Greek moussaka.

SERRANO HAM INFO

Unlike Iberian ham, this air-dried **Spanish ham** is obtained solely from light-skinned, domestic pigs. It is notable for its non-fibrous, lean flesh. It is rubbed

with sea salt and dried for at least 12 months. It used to be dried exclusively in the hills ("sierra" in Spanish), from which it derived its name.

Serves 4

2	eggplant
	Salt
4 tbsp	oil
1	onion, chopped
2	garlic cloves, chopped
14 oz (400 g)	canned tomatoes
	Pepper
1 tsp	dried thyme
10	slices Serrano ham
10	slices Gouda or Manchego cheese
1/2 bunch	basil, shredded

Step by step

Halve the eggplant lengthwise, sprinkle with salt, and leave for 15 minutes to draw out the bitter juices.

Wash and pat dry the eggplant slices, then place 1 slice ham and 1 slice cheese on each slice of eggplant.

Heat the oil in a pan and, stirring continuously, sweat the onion and garlic until transparent.

Roll up the eggplant and secure with toothpicks, then place in an ovenproof dish. Pour over the tomato sauce.

Add the tomatoes, season with salt, pepper, and thyme, and simmer for 15 minutes.

Bake in the oven at 400 °F/200 °C for 45 minutes. Garnish with shredded basil.

EGGPLANT
rolls in tomato sauce

SIDE DISHES
for eggplant

You will find the perfect side dishes for our eggplant recipes here.

Rice with dried fruit

Sweat 1¹/₄ cups (250 g) basmati rice, then cook in salt water. Sauté raisins, chopped figs, and dates in butter. Fold into the cooked rice. Season to taste with salt, cinnamon, and nutmeg. Goes well with eggplant au gratin, and stuffed eggplant.

Goat's cheese gratin

Combine crushed fennel with chopped thyme and honey, and spread onto slices of goat's cheese. Broil for 7 minutes. Goes well with the purée, and rolls in tomato sauce variations.

Pilaf with meat

Brown a chopped onion with sliced mushrooms and strips of lamb. Add diced tomatoes. Pour over bouillon, stir in rice, and cook. Season with salt and pepper, and stir in chopped nuts. Goes well with ratatouille.

... au gratin, with pesto, and mozzarella

Cut 4 eggplant lengthwise into slices. Place on a baking sheet, drizzle over 4 tablespoons olive oil, and bake in the oven at 400 °F/200 °C for 4 minutes. Brush with pesto, top with mozzarella slices, and brown under the broiler.

... as a purée, with olives

Sauté 1³/₄ lb (800 g) peeled, diced eggplant with 3 oz (75 g) diced onion and 2 chopped garlic cloves in 4 tablespoons olive oil. Drizzle over 2 tablespoons white wine vinegar. Add ³/₄ cup (175 ml) light cream, season with salt and pepper, and cook for 15 minutes. Purée. Combine with 1³/₄ oz (50 g) diced sun-dried tomatoes, 1 chopped red chile, and chopped parsley. Serve with pitted, sliced black olives.

EGGPLANT
several variations

Purple eggplant tastes quite boring when it is cooked by itself. In our variations, however, it is prepared in the right way to create some wonderful dishes when combined with other ingredients.

... with ground meat, as moussaka

Fry generous 1 lb (500 g) ground meat with 1 each chopped onion and garlic clove. Add generous 1 lb (500 g) diced tomatoes with 1 cup (250 ml) white wine, salt, $\frac{1}{2}$ teaspoon cinnamon, and pepper. Add 2 tablespoons each chopped mint and parsley. Fold in $3\frac{1}{2}$ oz (100 g) each breadcrumbs and grated cheese. Place 14 oz (400 g) fried eggplant slices in an ovenproof dish with the ground meat. Top with béchamel sauce. Bake at 350 °F/180 °C for 45 minutes.

... stuffed with mushrooms

Halve 4 eggplant, salt, and bake at 350 °F/180 °C for 25 minutes. Leave to cool. Remove the flesh, and chop up small. Sweat with $3\frac{1}{2}$ oz (100 g) each diced chanterelles and common-store mushrooms. Season with salt and pepper, then fold in 3 tablespoons each grated Ricotta and milk, 1 tablespoon chopped oregano, and $\frac{1}{4}$ cup (30 g) grated Parmesan. Spoon into the eggplant halves. Bake in the oven for about 10 minutes.

... with zucchini, and tomatoes in ratatouille

Sweat 2 chopped onions and 2 chopped garlic cloves in oil. Dice $1\frac{1}{4}$ lb (600 g) each eggplant, zucchini, and skinned tomatoes. Add to the onions and simmer. Add 1 bay leaf, 2 tablespoons herbes de Provence, salt, and pepper, and pour over 2 cups (500 ml) white wine. Simmer for about 15 minutes until soft.

... marinated with basil

Slice 2 eggplant. Sprinkle with salt and set aside. Drain and squeeze out the juices. Simmer in 2 cups (500 ml) white wine vinegar with 4 peeled garlic cloves for 5 minutes. Remove and drain thoroughly. Arrange in alternate layers with 20 basil leaves in glass jars. Top with peppercorns, cayenne, 1 cup (250 ml) olive oil, and salt. Leave for 8 days.

SALSIFY
in butter

Serves 4

generous 1 lb (500 g)	salsify Vinegar Salt
¹/₃ cup (75 g)	butter Freshly grated nutmeg Pepper

Step by step

Brush the salsify thoroughly, then peel and cut into pieces of equal sizes.

Slowly melt the butter in a skillet; do not allow it to brown.

Place immediately in a bowl of vinegar water to prevent discoloration.

Put the salsify in the skillet and coat in the butter.

Cook the salsify in boiling salt water for 15–20 minutes. Remove with a slotted spoon, and set aside.

Finally, season the salsify with nutmeg and pepper.

SALSIFY INFO

Salsify is sometimes referred to as winter asparagus, because of its shape and its peak season of November through March. Because its delicate flavor is reminiscent of oysters, salsify is

also known as oyster plant. Salsify is available in black or white varieties. The roots are not as easy to handle as the delicate stalks of the spring, however. The black skin contains a resinous juice that makes peeling them laborious, and leaves the fingers sticky and black. So it is best to wear kitchen gloves for this job. As the roots also oxidize (turn brown) quickly, the salsify should be placed in a bowl of lemon or vinegar water as soon as it has been peeled. A few dashes of lemon juice or vinegar should also be added to the cooking water; do not allow the salsify to become too soft. Treat it as asparagus in all other respects. It is delicious in soups and stews, with creamy sauces, baked and au gratin, breaded, and in salads. Salsify goes with all kinds of meat, game, poultry, and fish, and combines beautifully with other vegetables such as potatoes, leeks, celeriac, and spinach.

125

SALSIFY
s e v e r a l   v a r i a t i o n s

This lovely vegetable is often seriously underestimated. With its subtle flavor, salsify is much like asparagus, and can be prepared in the same way.

... as soup, with shrimp

Cook 1$^1/_2$ lb (700 g) diced salsify in 3$^1/_3$ cups (800 ml) vegetable bouillon for about 20 minutes. Remove one-quarter of the vegetables. Stir in 3$^1/_3$ cups (800 ml) light cream and 3 table-spoons cold butter. Season to taste with salt, pepper, cayenne, and nutmeg. Return the removed vegetables to the soup. Heat 7 oz (200 g) shrimp in the soup. Sprinkle with croutons.

... au gratin

Trim and peel generous 1 lb (500 g) salsify and cut into small pieces. Cook in salt water for about 20 minutes, until soft. Make a béchamel sauce from butter, flour, bouillon, and milk, and pour over the drained salsify pieces. Season with pepper and nutmeg. Sprinkle over scant 1 cup (100 g) grated Parmesan, and brown under the broiler.

... au gratin, with oyster mushrooms

Sweat 2 chopped shallots and 14 oz (400 g) diced oyster mushrooms, and season with salt, pepper, and nutmeg. Fold in 6 tablespoons (50 g) chopped, roasted pine nuts. Make a cream sauce with 3$^1/_2$ oz (100 g) cream cheese. Layer 2$^1/_4$ lb (1 kg) cooked salsify, mushrooms, and sauce in an ovenproof dish. Sprinkle with diced sun-dried tomatoes and grated Parmesan. Bake at 400 °F/200 °C for 40 minutes.

... with ground meat, in a vegetable wrap

Brush 8 ready to cook tortillas with sour cream. Fill with generous 1 lb (500 g) fried mixed ground meat, 1 chopped onion, 2 sliced carrots, 7 oz (200 g) salsify cut into thin sticks, 5 oz (140 g) sweet corn, and 3$^1/_2$ oz (100 g) sliced white cabbage cooked in vegetable bouillon. Season with salt, pepper, and ground chile, and roll into sausage shapes. Sprinkle with cheese, and bake at 425 °F/220 °C for 10 minutes.

SIDE DISHES
for salsify

If you like salsify, despite the effort required for preparing it, then try it with one of these side dishes.

Mashed celery

Cook 14 oz (400 g) each potatoes and celery until soft. Push the potatoes through a ricer. Fold in the chopped celery. Top with salt, pepper, nutmeg, and chopped parsley. Goes well with the vegetables, au gratin, and ragout variations.

Brown bread dumplings

Soak day-old brown bread in warm milk, and knead to a dough with butter, 1 egg, cumin, dried marjoram, salt, pepper, and nutmeg. Shape into dumplings and cook in salt water. Goes well with the vegetables recipe, and with the soup instead of croutons.

Ham and potato cakes

Grate 1³/₄ lb (800 g) raw potatoes and combine with finely chopped boiled ham, parsley, egg yolk, flour, and sesame seeds. Form into little patties and fry in hot oil.

... as ragout with morels

Soak 1 oz (25 g) dried morels and reserve the soaking water. Cook 1³/₄ lb (800 g) trimmed, chopped salsify for 20 minutes until soft. Make a roux from 4 tablespoons butter and 2 tablespoons flour. Add generous ³/₄ cup (200 ml) each light cream, the mushroom water, and the salsify cooking water, and simmer until creamy. Add the chopped morels, salt, pepper, and nutmeg, and sprinkle with chopped parsley.

... caramelized with young spinach

Caramelize 1³/₄ lb (800 g) cooked, diced salsify in a pan with 1 chopped red chile and 3 tablespoons honey. Season with salt, then cook until creamy with ³/₄ cup (175 ml) vegetable bouillon. Add 3 tablespoons vinegar. Combine with 5¹/₂ oz (150 g) grated celeriac, 3 tablespoons (20 g) chopped walnuts, and 7 oz (200 g) young spinach leaves, cut into strips. Pour over a dressing of olive oil, vinegar, salt, and pepper.

WINTER

In winter, we start to look forward to delicious cabbages in red, white, and green and to savoy cabbage and Brussels sprouts; the latter taste particularly good after the first frost.

They are all chock-full of vitamins, which make them particularly good for this cold time of year.

Chicory is another winter vegetable, and you'll be amazed by its versatility.

SAVOY CABBAGE INFO

Savoy cabbage is a member of the brassica family. Its versatility makes it one of the most popular cabbage varieties. Its intense flavor can be softened, if desired, by the addition of cream or a

pinch of sugar. The leaves of fresh savoy cabbage should be dark green on the outside, light green through yellow on the inside, and feel crisp to the touch. Like all cabbages and kales, savoy cabbage is full of vitamins and minerals. It contains lots of calcium and vitamin C.

SHALLOTS INFO

Shallots are considered the nobility of the alliums, which also include the common onion.

Shallots (échalote in French) have a much milder, more delicate flavor than their big sisters, which makes them the best choice in recipes that call for raw onions. Shallot butter goes beautifully with grilled or barbecued meat and canapés.

Serves 4

2¹/₄ lb (1 kg)	savoy cabbage
	Salt
3 tbsp	butter
2	shallots, chopped
1 tbsp	flour
1 cup (250 ml)	light cream
	Pepper
	Nutmeg

Step by step

Remove any limp leaves from the cabbage, and cut the stalk out in a cone shape.

Combine the cream and a generous ³/₄ cup (200 ml) of the cabbage water.

Boil the cabbage in salt water for 20 minutes. Drain (retaining a little of the liquid), and finely chop. Cut the cabbage into pieces.

Add the cabbage and cook for about 30 minutes.

Melt the butter and sweat the finely chopped shallots until transparent. Dust with the flour.

Season with salt, pepper, and freshly grated nutmeg.

SAVOY CABBAGE
in cream with shallots

SAVOY CABBAGE
several variations

Savoy cabbage is more versatile than you might have imagined. Here are six delicious recipes. They range from the classic, stuffed cabbage leaves, to unusual versions with morels.

... roulade with mushrooms and pork

Take 8 large, blanched savoy cabbage leaves, and place 2 together. Fill with a mixture of 14 oz (400 g) sliced pork medallions seasoned with salt, pepper, and oregano, $5^1/_2$ oz (150 g) diced shallots, chopped parsley, sautéed shiitake, and a little chopped garlic. Tie up in little parcels. Cover with bacon rashers and simmer in a little vegetable bouillon for about 40 minutes.

... pot-au-feu with lamb

Cook $2^1/_4$ lb (1 kg) diced lamb shoulder, 1 savoy cabbage cut into 4 pieces, 4 diced onions, 4 chopped potatoes, 4 chopped carrots, chopped parsley roots, chopped leek, chopped celeriac and celery stalks, salt, 12 peppercorns, 2 bay leaves, 2 cloves, fresh rosemary, and grated lemon rind in water for $1^1/_2$ hours. Remove the bay leaf before serving.

... puréed with cream

Sweat 4 finely chopped shallots in 2 tablespoons oil until soft. Add $2^1/_4$ lb (1 kg) blanched finely chopped savoy cabbage and 7 tablespoons (100 ml) each light cream and milk. Season with salt, white pepper, and nutmeg. Cook for 15 minutes. Add 2 tablespoons butter. Blend the savoy cabbage with a handheld blender. Bind with cornstarch if required.

... as a piquant pie with bacon

Pastry: $1^3/_4$ cups (250 g) flour, 1 egg, $8^1/_2$ tablespoons (125 g) butter. Roll out and use to line a pie plate. Sauté the bacon until the fat runs, then add 1 each chopped onion and garlic clove, and sweat until soft. Fold in generous 1 lb (500 g) sliced, blanched savoy cabbage. Season with salt, pepper, and nutmeg. Combine generous $3/_4$ cup (200 g) crème fraîche and 1 egg, and smooth over the pie. Sprinkle over the diced bacon and cheese. Bake at 350 °F/180 °C for 20 minutes.

FILLINGS
for savoy cabbage

Why not try one of these three fillings for savoy cabbage leaves? The preparation is the same as given for the roulade at the top of page 132.

... with lime juice, ginger, and soy sauce

Sweat 2 diced shallots and 2 in. (5 cm) finely chopped ginger in 4 tablespoons sesame oil. Add 2¼ lb (1 kg) finely chopped and blanched savoy cabbage, and simmer for 5 minutes. Pour in 7 table spoons (100 ml) rice wine, and cook until the cabbage is al dente. Season with soy sauce, lime juice, salt, pepper, and maple syrup.

... with morels

Chop 9 oz (250 g) fresh (or 1¾ oz/50 g dried) morels into small pieces. Sauté in a wok with melted herb butter and 1 chopped garlic clove and 1 teaspoon sesame seeds. Add 1¾ lb (800 g) blanched, thinly sliced savoy cabbage and cook for about 5 minutes, stirring continuously. Season with salt, soy sauce, and garam masala.

Savoy cabbage roulade Mediterranean style

Combine saffron rice, diced tomatoes, sautéed diced onion, and grated Parmesan. Season with salt, lemon juice, and chopped chervil.

Savoy cabbage roulade with shrimp farci

Purée cleaned, raw shrimp, salt, cayenne, and 3 tablespoons each light cream and crème fraîche. Season to taste with sherry. Stir in chopped scallions.

Savoy cabbage roulade Asian style

Sweat bamboo shoots and grated carrots in ghee, and steam bean sprouts. Add soy sauce. Season with pepper, cumin, and turmeric.

WHITE CABBAGE
b r a i s e d   w i t h   b a c o n

INFO

White cabbage is generally considered to be only for winter. This is not really the case, however, since it is available fresh all year round. It contains more vitamins than almost any other variety of cabbage, either raw or cooked. White cabbage goes with fried, grilled, and braised pork, lamb, and mutton; sausages, hamburgers, and Mettwurst.

Serves 4

2¹/₄ lb (1 kg)	white cabbage
7 oz (200 g)	smoked belly pork, diced
3 tbsp	clarified butter
1	onion, diced
¹/₂ cup (125 ml)	white wine
¹/₂ cup (125 ml)	vegetable bouillon
2 tsp	cumin seeds
	Salt
	Pepper
	Sugar

Step by step

Cut the cabbage into quarters. Remove any wilted leaves and the core, and grate very finely.

Fry the diced belly pork in 1 tablespoon of clarified butter. Set aside for a few moments.

Sauté the onion in 2 tablespoons of clarified butter in a casserole.

Stir in the belly pork with the fat, and add the white cabbage.

Add the wine, vegetable bouillon, and cumin, and season with salt and pepper. Simmer for 30–40 minutes. Season to taste with sugar.

Side dish

A coarse **bratwurst** goes well with braised cabbage. Slit the sausages in a few places and fry them all over in oil until brown and crispy.

Bratwurst can also be broiled. Pierce the skins first, so that the fat drips out as they cook.

Side dish

Boiled potatoes perfectly complement a meal of braised cabbage and bratwurst. Peel and halve $1^3/_4$ lb (800 g) potatoes, and cook in a little salted water for about 20 minutes. Drain and cool until no longer steaming. Drizzle over a little of the sausage juices, and serve with the cabbage and sausages.

135

SAUCES
for white cabbage

Celery and sherry, bacon, and mango and chile are the ingredients for these sauces for white cabbage.

Celery and sherry sauce
Simmer and reduce steamed diced onion and celery with dried thyme and sherry. Pour over some vegetable bouillon, and simmer. Stir in a mixture of cornstarch and sherry. Season with balsamic vinegar, honey, salt, and pepper.

Bacon sauce
Combine some shallots and diced bacon in butter with flour and wine. Pour over vegetable bouillon, and season with salt, pepper, and light cream. Bind with butter and a little cornstarch.

Mango and chile chutney
Sauté shallot and chopped chile. Stir in some ready-made mango chutney and chopped cilantro.

WHITE CABBAGE
several

People have mixed views about white cabbage. In bygone days, a large cabbage stew would be cooked on Monday and made to last for the rest of the week, so it has an association with poverty. On the other hand, many of those seeking to lose weight swear nowadays by the "cabbage diet." Whatever

... stuffed cabbage leaves
Blanch 8 cabbage leaves, and layer 2 together in 4 little stacks. Filling: combine 14 oz (400 g) onion, $1/2$ cup (100 g) cooked rice, 1 egg, 4 tablespoons thinly sliced olives, 2 chopped anchovies, and 2 tablespoons grated Parmesan. Brown the roulades in butter. Stir in 2 teaspoons tomato paste, $1/4$ teaspoon ground paprika, and $1/2$ cup (125 ml) meat bouillon. Simmer for 30 minutes.

... in a stew with potatoes and Mettwurst
Fry $1^3/4$ oz (50 g) diced bacon until the fat runs, then add 1 chopped garlic clove, 14 oz (400 g) thinly grated white cabbage, and 7 oz (200 g) cherry tomatoes. Stir in 14 oz (400 g) diced potatoes. Pour over $4^1/2$ cups (1.25 l) vegetable bouillon. Season with salt, pepper, and nutmeg. Cook for 20 minutes. Add 4 Mettwurst, and cook for a further 10 minutes.

variations

your view, however, it really is worth giving this vegetable a chance. These variations will show you why. The classic cabbage dish is without doubt the cabbage roulade, or stuffed cabbage leaves. However, it is also delicious as a strudel, in a stew, and with tagliatelle as "Krautfleckerl," an Austrian favorite.

... as a strudel in pastry

Make strudel pastry from 1³/₄ cups (250 g) flour, 1 pinch salt, ¹/₂ cup (125 ml) warm water, and 5 tablespoons oil. Roll out thinly. Sweat 1³/₄ oz (50 g) diced bacon, 1 diced onion, and 2 chopped garlic cloves. Sprinkle over 1 teaspoon sugar. Add 11 oz (300 g) sliced white cabbage. Wrap in strudel pastry. Bake at 350 °F/180 °C for about 1 hour.

... with tagliatelle as Krautfleckerl

Cook generous 1 lb (500 g) tagliatelle until al dente. Add 2 tea-spoons salt and 2 teaspoons cumin to 1¹/₄ lb (600 g) finely grated white cabbage. Leave to stand for 30 minutes, then squeeze out the juices. Sweat 1 diced onion in 6 tablespoons oil with 2 tablespoons sugar. Stir in the cabbage. Season with salt and ground paprika. Simmer until soft. Stir in the tagliatelle. Sprinkle with crispy bacon pieces before serving.

SAUCES
for white cabbage

Sauces with meat and sausages go well with cabbage strudel and stuffed cabbage leaves.

Cured pork sauce

Sauté leek, onion, and mushrooms. Stir in tomato paste. Pour over wine and bouillon, and reduce. Add chopped cured pork, and season to taste with salt, pepper, and chile powder.

Ham sauce

Brown chopped ham and onion in butter. Stir in light cream, egg, and milk. Season with salt, pepper, and nutmeg. Goes well with braised cabbage, and stuffed cabbage leaves.

Ground meat and cream sauce

Brown chopped onion and garlic with 9 oz (250 g) ground meat. Pour over bouillon, wine, and cream, and simmer. Season to taste with salt and pepper. Stir in some parsley.

SAUERKRAUT
simmered in Riesling

Serves 4

3 tbsp	*goose fat*
1	*onion, halved and sliced*
1	*clove garlic, chopped*
1 tsp	*cumin seeds*
1³/₄ lb (750 g)	*sauerkraut*
1	*bay leaf*
2	*cloves*
4	*juniper berries*
1 cup (250 ml)	*Riesling*
1–2 cups (250–500 ml)	*vegetable bouillon*
3 stalks	*parsley (leaves only)*

Step by step

Heat the goose fat in a pan. Sweat the onion and garlic with the cumin until transparent.

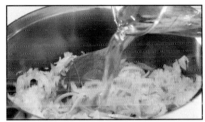

Add enough vegetable broth to cover the sauerkraut by about ³/₄ in. (2 cm).

Add the sauerkraut and simmer briefly, stirring continuously.

Cook the sauerkraut for a further 40–50 minutes, until soft.

Add the spices and wine. Cook for 10 minutes.

Sprinkle with chopped parsley leaves to serve.

SIDE DISHES
for sauerkraut

Spicy sauerkraut, patties, or puff pastry parcels all taste even better with a refreshing dip. Add cured pork and potato purée, and you really can't go wrong!

Potato purée with nuts

Make a purée of 1³/₄ lb (800 g) mealy potatoes, milk, butter, salt, pepper, and nutmeg, and finish with the chopped nuts of your choice.

Cured pork

Simmer sliced cured pork with the sauerkraut, or else sauté in a little oil in a skillet, and cut into cubes.

Mustard and curry dip

Combine mayonnaise, yogurt, and mustard, and stir until smooth. Add curry powder to taste. Season with salt and pepper. Fold in some chopped parsley. Goes well with gratin, patties, and puff pastry.

... with pineapple

Simmer 1³/₄ lb (750 g) sauerkraut with 4 juniper berries and 1 cup (250 ml) white wine for 30 minutes. Stir in 2 heaped tablespoons goose dripping, and simmer for a further 20 minutes. Stir in 1 tablespoon goose dripping and 9 oz (250 g) chopped, fresh pineapple. Simmer for a further 15 minutes. Season with a pinch of chile powder, if desired.

... as patties with potatoes and bacon

Combine 11 oz (300 g) cooked potatoes pushed through a ricer, 11 oz (300 g) well-squeezed white wine sauerkraut, 1 egg yolk, 7 oz (200 g) fried chopped bacon, and 1 tablespoon cornstarch. Season to taste with cayenne. Shape into patties and fry in hot fat until golden.

SAUERKRAUT
several variations

Although this lacto-fermented cabbage has a very strong flavor, it can be reduced or complemented by adding certain ingredients. Why not try one of these six variations:

... as soup with cured pork

Sweat 1 diced onion in 2 tablespoons lard, until soft. Then add 18 oz (500 g) finely chopped, squeezed sauerkraut, and simmer for 2 minutes. Add 14 oz (400 g) diced cured pork, 1 large mealy potato, chopped small, 1 bay leaf, 1 teaspoon cumin, a little white pepper, and 4 cups (1 liter) meat bouillon. Cook for 45 minutes. Stir in 4 tablespoons sour cream.

... with bell pepper and sour cream

Cook 1³/₄ lb (750 g) sauerkraut with 1 bay leaf, 1 clove, 4 juniper berries, and a little salt in bouillon until soft. Sauté 3¹/₂ oz (100 g) spicy sausage, 1 onion, and 1 red bell pepper (all finely chopped) in oil. Stir in 2 tablespoons tomato paste, 1 teaspoon ground paprika, and generous ³/₄ cup (200 ml) sour cream. Add to the sauerkraut. Mix thoroughly

... as puff pastry parcels with sausage

Roll 4 sheets puff pastry out as thinly as possible, and spread with butter. Top each one with 5¹/₂ oz (150 g) very finely chopped, well squeezed, white wine sauerkraut and 1 beef sausage. Fold the edge under and roll the pastry up. Brush with egg yolk and bake at 400 °F/200 °C for about 25 minutes.

... au gratin, with chestnuts, and buckwheat groats

Layer 14 oz (400 g) sauerkraut, 7 oz (200 g) chestnuts, lightly browned in butter, and buckwheat groats cooked in 2 cups (500 ml) vegetable bouillon in an ovenproof dish. Drizzle with melted butter and bake at 400 °F/200 °C for about 15 minutes, until golden.

CHICORY
au gratin, with ham

INFO

These crispy perennials have only been with us since the 19th century. They were first discovered in Belgium's Botanic Gardens. **Chicory** is the second bud of the chicory plant, so it is actually a shoot. The light green through white vegetables grow in the dark. Once you get them home, store them in a dark place. If the tips turn green, this indicates that they have had too much light. They can be eaten raw in salads, braised, grilled, or steamed.

Serves 4

4	chicory
2 cups (500 ml)	vegetable bouillon
	Salt
1/2 tsp	ground sweet paprika
2 tbsp	lime juice
8	small slices peppered ham
	Butter for the pan
3 1/2 oz (100 g)	Manchego, grated
2 tbsp	dried breadcrumbs
6	flakes butter

Step by step

Trim the chicory. Cut out the bitter core and cook in the vegetable bouillon until semi-soft.

Halve the chicory and season with salt and sweet paprika. Drizzle with the lime juice.

Wrap 1 slice ham around each chicory half, and place side by side in a buttered ovenproof dish.

Mix the grated Manchego with the breadcrumbs and scatter evenly over the top.

Dot with the butter flakes and bake at 400 °F/200 °C for 10–15 minutes, until golden.

Sauce

If you are serving chicory with poultry, then a **curry sauce** goes very well with, for instance, fried chicken or turkey breast. Stir 1 tablespoon curry powder into the chicken juices and simmer. Add 3 tablespoons hot bouillon. Combine $^2/_3$ cup (150 ml) milk with 2 teaspoons cornstarch and stir into the boiling sauce. Reduce slightly. Season with salt and pepper.

Side dish

Parsley rice goes very well with chicory, chicken, and curry sauce. Sweat $1^1/_4$ cups (250 g) rice in butter with a finely chopped shallot. Pour over 2 cups (500 ml) chicken broth, and cook the rice until al dente. Stir in some chopped parsley. Spoon the cooked rice into individual bowls, and serve with the sauce.

CHICORY
several variations

Chicory isn't just for salads. The fresh, vitamin-rich heads can also be prepared as a vegetable, filled with meat, fried with fish, or wrapped in bacon and browned under the broiler.

... with chicken breasts

Cut 1¼ lb (600 g) chicken breasts into strips and brown in 2 tablespoons olive oil. Cook 4 thickly sliced chicory heads in 1 cup (250 ml) chicken broth until still slightly al dente. Season with salt, pepper, and chopped sage. Add the chicken with 7 tablespoons (100 ml) light cream and 7 tablespoons (50 g) chopped walnuts. Reduce slightly.

... stuffed with ground meat and capers

Halve 4 chicory heads. Finely chop the inside leaves, leaving 3 outer leaves intact, and sweat the chopped leaves in butter with 1 diced onion. Combine with 7 oz (200 g) ground meat, 1 tablespoon capers, 1 egg, ½ bunch chopped parsley, salt, pepper, 1 teaspoon ground paprika, and 1 pinch nutmeg. Use to fill the hollowed-out chicory heads, sprinkle with dried breadcrumbs, and bake at 350 °F/180 °C in ½ cup (125 ml) white wine for 45 minutes.

... with cheese and cream sauce

Cook 4 chicory heads in salt water with a little lemon juice until just al dente. To make the sauce, combine 2 tablespoons flour in 2 tablespoons melted butter, then stir in 1 cup (250 ml) meat bouillon, 7 tablespoons (100 ml) light cream, and a scant cup (100 g) grated pecorino. Season with salt, cayenne, and 1 teaspoon chopped chervil. Simmer gently for 5 minutes. Pour over the drained chicory.

... oven-braised with fish fillets

Cut 4 chicory heads into 12 equal slices, and place side by side in an ovenproof dish. Cut 14 oz (400 g) cod fillet into 12 strips, and place one on top of each chicory slice. Season with salt and pepper, then drizzle with lemon juice, and bake at 425 °F/220 °C for 15 minutes. For the sauce, stir together 1 egg yolk, 1 tablespoon lemon juice, and 2 tablespoons white wine, then heat. Beat in 8½ tablespoons (120 g) butter.

SIDE DISHES
for chicory

Rice, potato chips, vegetables au gratin... chicory can be served with lots of different side dishes.

Rice and fruit

Cook 1¼ cups (250 g) rice in double the amount of water, until just al dente. Fold in chopped fresh fruit. Good choices include mixed berries, pineapple, pitted cherries, oranges, pitted dates, and papaya. Goes well with the cheese and cream sauce, and cheese and bacon recipe variations.

Potato, carrot, and tomato au gratin

Layer slices of potato, carrot, beefsteak tomatoes, and grated mozzarella in an ovenproof dish. Season light cream with salt, pepper, and marjoram, and pour over the potatoes. Bake until golden. Goes well with the meat stuffing recipe.

Potato chips

Thinly slice 1¾ lb (800 g) peeled, raw potatoes. Pat dry. Fry on both sides in hot oil until crispy. Sprinkle with salt, pepper, and chopped chervil. Goes well with all versions.

... broiled in cheese and bacon

Cook 4 chicory in salt water with a little lemon juice until just al dente. Cut in half. Grate a little pepper over each cut surface, drizzle with lemon juice, and spread thinly with mild mustard. Place two halves together, then wrap in slices of cheese and bacon. Broil until the cheese melts.

... in an Asian stir-fry

Blanch 1¼ lb (600 g) sliced chicory, 7 oz (200 g) frozen peas, and 11 oz (300 g) slivered almonds. Heat 6 tablespoons oil and sweat 11 oz (300 g) chopped shallots. Add the drained carrots, peas, and chicory. Stir in the grated rind and juice of 1 lime, 2 teaspoons grated ginger, 1 tablespoon brown sugar, 2 chopped red chiles, 3 tablespoons soy sauce, 1 tablespoon wine, 1 teaspoon cornstarch, 1–2 tablespoons oyster sauce, and a little water.

BRUSSELS SPROUTS
steamed with walnuts

Serves 4

2 lb (900 g)	*Brussels sprouts*
1 cup (250 ml)	*vegetable bouillon*
2	*shallots*
1	*clove garlic*
3 tbsp	*butter*
5 stalks	*fresh thyme or cilantro, chopped*
7 tbsp (50 g)	*walnuts, chopped*
	Salt
	Pepper
	Nutmeg

Step by step

Remove any limp leaves from the Brussels sprouts. Trim the base. Wash the sprouts and cut a cross into the base.

Sweat the shallots with the garlic in butter until transparent.

Cook the Brussels sprouts in the vegetable bouillon for about 10 minutes, until slightly soft. Pour off the water, and leave to drain.

Stir in the Brussels sprouts. Cover and simmer for 5 minutes.

Finely chop the shallots and garlic.

Fold in the herbs and walnuts, and season to taste. Simmer for another 2 minutes.

SAUCES
for Brussels sprouts

The slight sweetness of the Brussels sprout harmonizes particularly well with these sauces.

Horseradish sauce

Make a roux from flour and butter, then add finely grated, fresh horseradish. Add vegetable bouillon, and reduce by one-third. Season with salt, pepper, and sugar, and finish with heavy cream. Goes well with the stir-fried vegetables, and au gratin variations.

Gorgonzola sauce

Make a roux. Add 2 cups (500 ml) milk, and reduce by one-third. Crumble in 3$\frac{1}{2}$ oz (100 g) Gorgonzola; melt. Season to taste with salt and pepper.

Mushroom and sherry sauce

Sauté sliced brown mushrooms and chopped shallots in butter. Deglaze with light cream and sherry, and reduce slightly. Fold in some chopped flat-leaf parsley.

BRUSSELS SPROUT
several

Brussels sprouts taste particularly delicious when they have had a frost, as it converts their starch into sugar. Of course, you can freeze fresh sprouts for 1–2 days instead, which has the same effect. Try these four variations: Brussels sprouts tart with goat's cheese; with bacon and cabanossi; au gratin,

... as a tart with goat's cheese

Combine 3 tablespoons each butter and milk, 1 egg yolk, $\frac{1}{2}$ teaspoon baking powder, and 1 pinch salt with $\frac{2}{3}$ cup (100 g) flour. Roll out thinly and line an 8-in. (20-cm) tart pan. Beat 1 egg with 3$\frac{1}{2}$ oz (100 g) goat's cheese, 11 oz (300 g) blanched and sliced Brussels sprouts, and 4 tablespoons each diced bacon and chopped tomatoes. Season with salt and pepper, and smooth over the pastry shell. Bake at 400 °F/200 °C for 15 minutes.

... au gratin, with filberts

Pour $\frac{1}{2}$ cup (125 ml) vegetable bouillon over sweated onion. Season with salt, pepper, and thyme. Leave to cool. Fold in generous $\frac{3}{4}$ cup (200 ml) light cream, 2 beaten eggs, $\frac{1}{2}$ bunch finely chopped parsley, and 1$\frac{3}{4}$ lb (800 g) blanched Brussels sprouts. Place in an ovenproof dish, then bake at 350 °F/180 °C for 40 minutes. Top with 7 tablespoons (50 g) chopped filberts and scant 1 cup (100 g) grated, sharp Cheddar and broil until golden.

variations

with sharp Cheddar; and in stir-fried vegetables with meatballs. These "little cabbages" also go extremely well with other vegetables and mushrooms.

SIDE DISHES
for Brussels sprouts

These three side dishes with potatoes and semolina go particularly well with Brussels sprouts.

Mini rösti

Peel 1³/₄ lb (800 g) cooked waxy potatoes, and grate coarsely. Combine with chopped ham and season with pepper. Shape into little patties and fry on both sides until golden.

... au gratin, with bacon, cabanossi, and Feta

Cook 1³/₄ lb (800 g) Brussels sprouts in vegetable bouillon until al dente, then place in an ovenproof dish. Top with 7 oz (200 g) diced cabanossi. Cut 3¹/₂ oz (100 g) smoked bacon rashers into strips, and layer on top in a grid pattern. Crumble over 7 oz (200 g) diced Feta, and drizzle with olive oil. Bake at 400 °F/200 °C until golden.

Fried herb polenta

Soak 1¹/₃ cups (200 g) cornmeal in twice the amount of vegetable bouillon, then stir in 2 tablespoons chopped herbs. Smooth onto a baking sheet, and allow to cool. Cut into slices, and fry in herb butter until golden.

... as stir-fry with rutabaga and carrots

Sweat 2 each chopped onions and garlic cloves in a skillet. Add 4 diced tomatoes, 1 cup (250 ml) vegetable bouillon, 14 oz (400 g) Brussels sprouts, and 7 oz (200 g) each rutabaga and carrots. Season with salt, pepper, and marjoram. Cook for about 20 minutes, until al dente.

Potato croquettes

Cook 1³/₄ lb (800 g) mealy potatoes in their skins, then peel and push through a ricer. Combine with 2 tablespoons butter, 1 egg yolk, and 1 tablespoon light cream, and season with salt, pepper, and nutmeg. Shape into cylinders, and coat in beaten egg, flour, and breadcrumbs. Deep fry in hot oil.

RED CABBAGE
w i t h   a p p l e

INFO

Red cabbage is actually a variety of the green cabbage, although its leaves are slightly tougher, and more bitter. This has led to a number of chefs using it to make sauerkraut—with great success. Botanically, **red cabbage** is, like all other brassicas, a hybrid. Red cabbage is most often cooked with apples, cloves, and juniper berries, and typically served with roast goose, game, and roast beef.

Serves 4

1	*large red cabbage (approx. 2¼ lb/1 kg)*
1	*red onion, chopped*
2 tbsp	*clarified butter*
2	*cloves*
1–2 tsp	*superfine sugar*
1 pinch	*nutmeg*
1 pinch	*Salt*
1 pinch	*black pepper*
3–4 tbsp	*apple vinegar*
7 tbsp	*apple juice*
1	*tart apple, peeled, grated, and sprinkled with lemon juice*

Step by step

Cut the red cabbage into quarters. Remove any limp leaves and the core, and cut very thinly.

Sweat the onion in hot clarified butter until transparent. Sprinkle with the sugar, and caramelize lightly.

Add the red cabbage, spices, and seasoning. Cook for 3 minutes, stirring continuously. Deglaze with apple vinegar and apple juice.

Add water, if required, and stir the grated apple into the red cabbage.

Simmer gently over low-medium heat for about 45 minutes. Season with lemon juice, salt, and pepper.

Side dish

Boiled potatoes garnished with a little parsley go well with red cabbage. **Spätzle** is another alternative. To make spätzle, combine scant 3 cups (400 g) flour with 4 eggs, milk, and a little salt to make a viscous dough, and stand for 20 minutes. To cook, push through a spätzle grater or press into boiling salted water. When the spätzle rise to the surface, remove with a slotted spoon; drain, and serve in a bowl.

Side dish

To make glazed **chestnuts**, bake generous 1 lb (500 g) chestnuts, with a cross cut into the base, in the oven for 15 minutes. Peel, making sure to remove the bitter, inner skin as well. Pour over ¹/₂ cup (125 ml) vegetable bouillon, then cover and simmer for about 10 minutes. Drain well. Caramelize 3 tablespoons sugar in 2 tablespoons butter, coat the chestnuts, and simmer for about 4 minutes.

SIDE DISHES
for red cabbage

As well as spätzle, various types of dumpling go well with red cabbage.

Bread dumplings

Combine butter-fried croutons, diced onion, finely chopped parsley, eggs, flour, salt, and milk, and knead until smooth. When ready to cook, roll up in a tea towel like a sausage, and tie. Cook for 20 minutes, then unwrap, and cut into slices.

Pretzel dumplings

Combine broken pretzels with eggs, warm milk, finely chopped parsley, sweated onions, salt, pepper, and nutmeg, and knead to make a malleable dough. Shape into dumplings and simmer in salt water for 20 minutes.

RED CABBAGE
several

If you have previously only ever had red cabbage with roast goose and dumplings, you will find these variations extremely informative. Incidentally—when presented raw in a salad, this immunity-boosting vegetable with its richly colored leaves has a lot to recommend it.

... Bohemian style with bacon

Put 2^1/$_4$ lb (1 kg) very thinly sliced red cabbage, 3 tablespoons vinegar, and 3 tablespoons water in a saucepan. Top with 6 sugar cubes, and cook for 15 minutes. Sauté 5^1/$_2$ oz (150 g) smoked bacon rashers, and add to the cabbage. Season with salt, pepper, ground cloves, and a little ground allspice.

... with pears and raisins

Sweat 1 onion in 2 tablespoons butter until soft. Add 2^1/$_4$ lb (1 kg) thinly sliced red cabbage, 1 large, roughly chopped pear, 1^3/$_4$ oz (50 g) raisins, and 1 cup (250 ml) white wine. Season to taste with salt, pepper, grated lemon rind, cinnamon, salt, nutmeg, and pear juice.

variations

Although naturally blue in color, it changes to a deep red if you add a little lemon juice or vinegar when cooking. Red cabbage goes well with a wide range of spices, and even with rosewater.

... with rosewater, cinnamon, and cumin

Sweat 2¼ lb (1 kg) very thinly sliced red cabbage in 2 tablespoons butter. Add 1 teaspoon rosewater and 1 cup (250 ml) water. Season with 1 clove and 1 good pinch each cumin, salt, and pepper. Finish with rosé wine vinegar and cinnamon.

... with star anise

Marinate 2¼ lb (1 kg) very thinly sliced red cabbage in a bowl with ½ cup (125 ml) red wine vinegar, 2 star anise, 1 bay leaf, and ¼ cinnamon stick, for about 3 hours. Lightly caramelize 1 finely chopped onion in 2 tablespoons clarified butter and 2 tablespoons sugar. Add the red cabbage and 1 cup (250 ml) red wine. Season to taste with salt.

SIDE DISHES
for red cabbage

If you want to make something a little more unusual for a special occasion, here are two wonderful side dishes.

Chestnut spätzle

Prepare the spätzle dough as explained on page 151. Substitute chestnut flour for half the wheat flour.

Bolete pasta

Make a pasta dough from flour, eggs, salt, and a little warm water. Soak, then squeeze and stir in 1¾ oz (50 g) finely chopped bolete. Prepare your chosen pasta.

KALE

with "Pinklewurst" sausage

Serves 4

3¹/₄ lb (1.5 kg)	*kale*
	Salt
1	*onion*
3 tbsp	*oatmeal*
²/₃ cup (150 g)	*clarified butter*
2 cups (500 ml)	*meat bouillon*
	Black pepper
	Sugar
14 oz (400 g)	*streaky bacon, chopped*
4	*Pinklewurst or similar sausages*

Step by step

Wash the kale thoroughly and remove the stalks. Blanch in boiling salt water for a few minutes.

Stir in the kale and meat bouillon. Season with salt, pepper, and a generous pinch of sugar.

Drain the kale and leave to cool, then chop coarsely with a large, sharp knife.

Stir the chopped bacon into the kale. Cook for 1 hour. Add more bouillon, if required.

Finely chop the onion, and sauté with the oatmeal in clarified butter until soft, but not brown.

Add the chopped sausages. Simmer for a further 30 minutes. Season with sugar and salt.

SIDE DISHES
for kale

Potatoes any style go perfectly with kale. Crispy fried, garlic, or mashed potatoes are just 3 of the many variations.

Fried potatoes

Cut cold potatoes, with skins or without, into $1/2$-in. (1-cm) slices. Sweat onions in olive oil until transparent. Add diced bacon and sliced potatoes, and sauté until the potatoes are crispy. Season with black pepper and marjoram. Goes well with the Pinklewurst, and other recipe variations.

Garlic potatoes

Cook some roughly chopped potatoes in salt water. Pour off the water. Place the pan back on the stove top for a short while, shaking it gently so that the remaining water evaporates. Melt butter in a skillet. Add finely chopped garlic, and sauté the potatoes for 5 minutes.

Mashed potatoes

Roughly mash hot, boiled potatoes. Fold in hot milk and a little melted herb or garlic butter, making sure the potato mix remains crumbly. Sprinkle with finely chopped herbs, bacon, or chopped pepperoni.

... with eggs and chorizo

Sweat $2^1/_4$ lb (1 kg) finely chopped kale with 2 diced onions and 2 chopped garlic cloves in lard. Pour over 1 cup (250 ml) each meat bouillon and white wine. Simmer for 20 minutes. Just before serving, briefly fry thinly sliced chorizo in the skillet. Place on the kale, and top with fried eggs seasoned with salt and ground paprika.

... with chestnuts and glazed potatoes

Brown $3^1/_2$ oz (100 g) diced bacon and 12 oz (350 g) peeled chestnuts in 1 tablespoon oil. Add $2^1/_4$ lb (1 kg) coarsely chopped kale and 2 cups (500 ml) vegetable bouillon. Season with salt, pepper, and cumin. Cook for 1 hour. Boil $1^1/_4$ lb (600 g) potatoes in salt water, then shape into balls, and fry in butter. Sprinkle over 2 tablespoons sugar, coat the potatoes, and continue frying until they are golden brown. Place on top of the kale mixture.

KALE
several variations

This tasty winter vegetable is far more versatile than you might think. Try these variations, and see for yourself. From spicy, through creamy, to fruity, there's something for every palate.

... au gratin, with potatoes

Sauté 2 diced onions in lard. Coat 2^1/$_4$ lb (1 kg) finely chopped kale in the lard. Season with salt and cumin. Beat 3 eggs with pepper, marjoram, and a generous ^{3}/$_4$ cup (200 ml) light cream. Layer the kale, thinly sliced potatoes, and 1^3/$_4$ cups (200 g) grated Gruyère cheese in an ovenproof dish, and pour over the egg and cream mix. Bake at 350 °F/180 °C for 40 minutes.

... as lasagna, with bolete

Sweat 3^1/$_2$ oz (100 g) diced shallots, 11 oz (300 g) each bolete and chopped tomatoes, and ^{1}/$_2$ bunch chopped parsley in butter. Season with salt, pepper, and lemon juice. Sweat generous 1 lb (500 g) chopped kale in 1 tablespoon butter. Season with salt and nutmeg. Alternate lasagna pasta sheets with layers of the mushroom mix and kale. Pour over béchamel sauce. Bake at 350 °F/180 °C for 45 minutes.

... in cream sauce

Sweat 1 chopped onion in olive oil until soft, but not brown. Add 2^1/$_4$ lb (1 kg) coarsely chopped kale, generous ^{3}/$_4$ cup (200 ml) cream, and ^{1}/$_2$ cup (125 ml) vegetable bouillon. Season with salt and pepper. Bring to a boil briefly, then simmer over low heat for 30 minutes. Season with lemon juice and ground cumin. Bind with cornstarch, if desired.

... with apples/pears

Sweat 1 onion in 2 tablespoons clarified butter until soft. Add 1^3/$_4$ lb (800 g) diced cured pork. Then add 2^1/$_4$ lb (1 kg) finely chopped kale and 1^2/$_3$ cups (400 ml) meat bouillon. Season with salt, pepper, pimento, and sugar. Cook for 45 minutes. Add 2 large, roughly chopped, firm pears. Continue cooking for a further 10–15 minutes.

Index of recipes

Index of recipes